500 of the

Weirdest & Wackiest

Web Sites

Series Editors: Colleen Collier, Lucy Dear, Nicki Mellows, Nikole Bamford
Research: Nick Daws, Linley Clode, Nikole Bamford
Additional Contributors: Keith Fyfe, Christine Pountney, Richard Skinner, Sue Curran, Sarah Wells, Ann Marangos
Page Design and Layout: Linley Clode
Cover Design: Sol Communications Ltd

Published by:
Lagoon Books
PO Box 311, KT2 5QW, UK
PO Box 990676, Boston, MA 02199, USA

www.thelagoongroup.com

ISBN: 1-904797-74-1

Printed in Thailand.

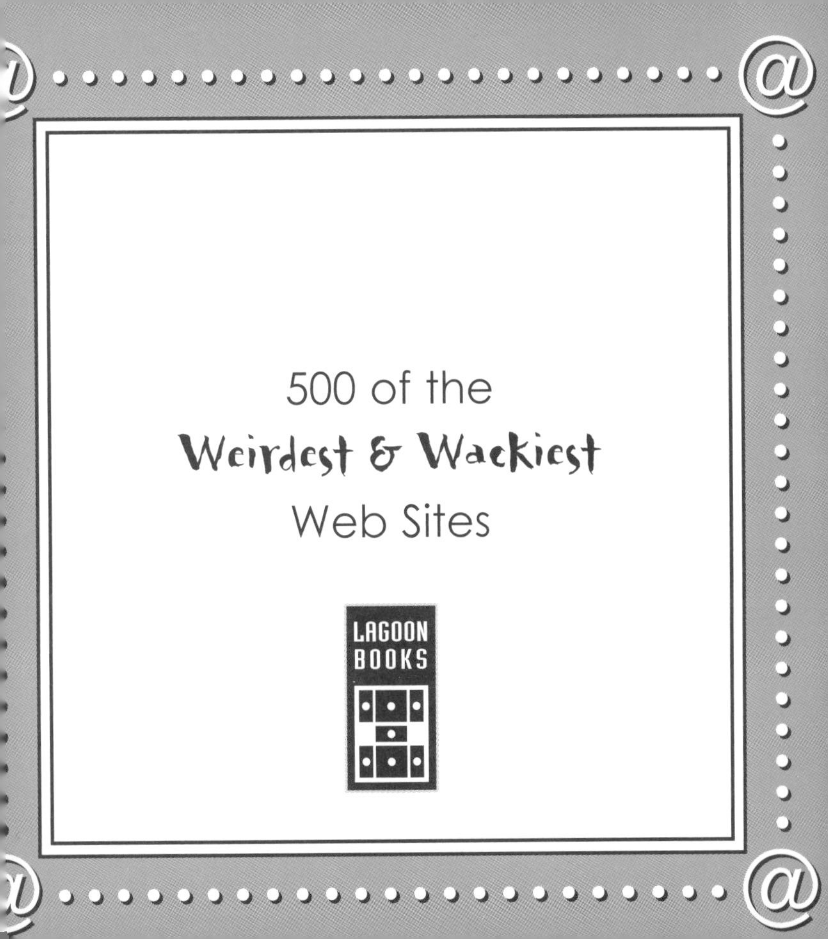
500 of the
Weirdest & Wackiest
Web Sites
LAGOON
BOOKS

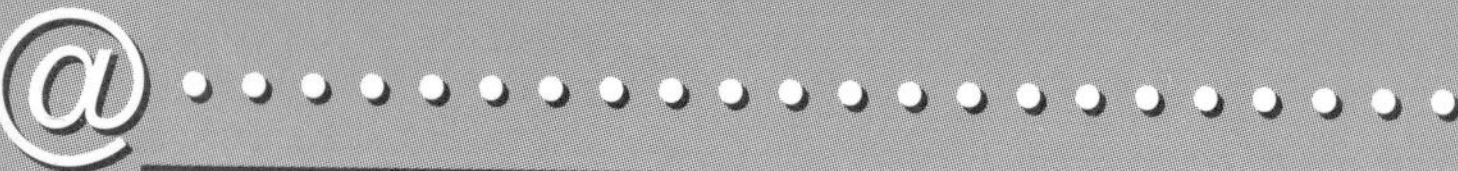

CONTENTS

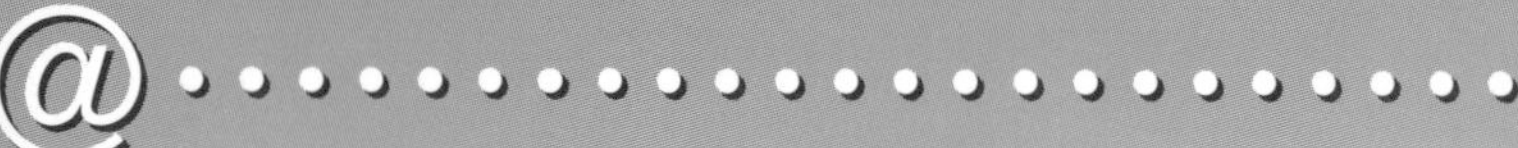

INTRODUCTION

'The Internet is a tidal wave...drowning those who don't learn to swim in its waves' – Bill Gates

Over the past few years, many guides to the Internet have been written explaining how to access the Net and how to use it. But now everyone's looking for a fun and easy-to-use guide to the best sites, so here it is!

This stunning 282-page directory lists 500 of the Weirdest & Wackiest Web Sites on the Internet and is subdivided into six amazing chapters according to subject to make searching even easier!

The research has been carried out by an avid team of fun-loving Internet surfers whose brief was to find the funniest and most original sites for you to enjoy – which is just what they did! Go to p41 or p143 to see what I mean!

Each site is listed with the web address and several lines of text, hinting at what you might find if you log on and visit the web site. The book is for all ages and abilities – you don't have to be a computer whizz or an Internet expert to use it.

Amongst the 500 fantastic web sites listed here, you will be able to find out...

...Where you can buy a million dollars for just $0.50
...How long you have left to live
...How to build your own computer...from scratch!
...Where your missing socks are hiding
...Whether or not you have been abducted by aliens
...Who owns a container filled with their own navel fluff
...What garbage top Hollywood stars have thrown out recently
...Where you can buy a piece of Mars
...Where you can read secret FBI files

It's amazing what people put on the Internet, so here is the ultimate guide to finding all that is silly, funny, ridiculous, creepy, weird and outrageous!

Get online for hours of fun and entertainment!

If it's weird and wacky, you'll find it here!

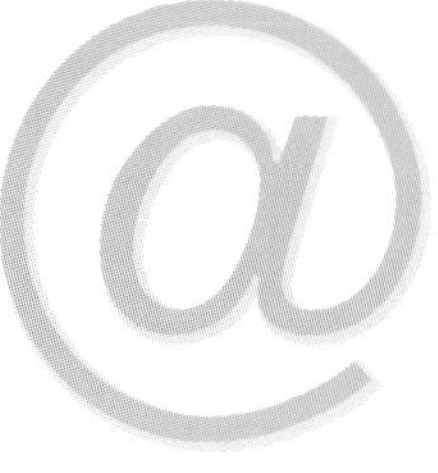

1

Silly, Funny and Ridiculous

The Subservient Chicken

http://www.subservientchicken.com

What could be more fun and relaxing than ordering a chicken about? Type your demands into the box provided and watch the poultry slave comply.

April Fools Online

http://www.wonderfullywacky.com

Don't know what to buy your boring aunt or uncle? Make their day with a Kung Fu Hamster, Moose Poop Candy Dispenser or Chocolate Body Painting Kit.

Love And Balloons

http://www.balloonhat.com

The home page of a couple of guys, who travel the world to make balloon hats for unhappy people, with photos of people wearing their balloon hats in 34 different countries!

Who Would Buy That?

http://www.whowouldbuythat.com

Stuff that surely nobody could ever want to own - just who DOES buy toilet paper that teaches you Japanese?

Cyber Stare

http://www.pixelscapes.com/spatulacity/stare2.htm

So you think you can out-stare anyone in a contest? Try this virtual reality staring contest...

The Mother-of-all-excuses Page

http://members.tripod.com/Madtbone

Divided into categories such as police, school, work, and breaking a date – this site offers a plethora of excuses. Perhaps you will want to submit your own gems?

Guess Who I Am!

http://www.smalltime.com/dictator.html

A simple online game where you pretend to be a sitcom character or a famous dictator and the computer tries to figure out who you are.

How To Get A Head In Advertising

http://www.headvertise.com

Short of cash? Why not rent your forehead out as a billboard? No doubt coming to a town near you shortly!

Pave the Planet

http://www.geocities.com/SouthBeach/1380/pave.html

This hilarious site has come up with the 'perfect' solution to all of our environmental problems – what do you think it is?

How To Dance Properly

http://www.zefrank.com/invite/swfs/index2.html

Men, in particular, can be guilty of some extremely bad dancing...but help is finally here in the shape of this hilarious site!

The Great Debate Page

http://www.angelfire.com/ct/tpdebate

Which way round should the toilet roll be hung? Which is best – sauce or gravy? A simple voting site on these and other extremely important issues. Make sure you have your say!

The Love Calculator

http://www.lovecalculator.com

'Do you love me 85 per cent?' 'Oh, then do you love me 76 per cent?'. Enter two names into the 'Love Calculator' and find out what your chances really are.

The Guy Card

http://www.guycard.com

Do you feel your right to be a guy is diminished in this modern world? Do you want to reclaim the right to dress like a guy, watch guy TV and generally do guy things? If you answered 'Yes' to any of these questions, you obviously need a 'Guy Card'.

Tip a Cow

http://www.nwlink.com/~timelvis/cowtip.html

Real-life cow-tipping is a dangerous and cruel prank – but at this site you can fulfil your desire to tip a virtual cow as many times as you like!

Just Chill Out

http://www.mezzowave.net/chillout.htm

When all the silliness gets too much, take a relaxing breather at the 'super-sensory chill-out lounge' on this cool site, with its cool online ambient music.

Large Furry Animals

http://www.nose-n-toes.com

Llamas aren't cute, are they? But, if you happen to know anyone who harbors the delusion that they are, you can order them any of a huge range of llama-themed merchandize from this site.

Shrink in a Box

http://www.dreamwv.com/shrink/shrink.html

Don't want to pay by the hour? Need a quick analysis? Visit the site, take a seat, the doctor will be with you shortly...

Python Online

http://www.pythonline.com

The official site of all things relating to the pythonesque world of 'Monty Python'. An absolute must for fans.

Free Cartoons

http://www.joecartoon.com

Download original animated cartoons to watch on your computer. Choose from a huge range, including Disco Mouse, Teenage Gerbil Bikers and Santa Yo' Daddy.

The Movie Nitpickers' Site

http://www.nitpickers.com

We've all seen them – those continuity mistakes, the out-of-sequence scenes where the empty glass has become full. Here's the site where you can register your own movie nitpick, or just peruse the massive archive of what other people have already noticed.

Stare Down Sally

http://www.stairwell.com/stare

Sally will blink...eventually! Do you think you're a match for her?

I Should be Working!

http://www.ishouldbeworking.com

But you're not, are you? Visit this site to enjoy amusing offerings from like-minded slackers.

Apology-note Generator

http://www.karmafarm.com/formletter.html

This web site takes all the effort out of finding the right words to say you're sorry – and when you're happy with your message, it will e-mail it to your beloved for you!

Useless Facts Page

http://www.uselessfacts.net

Useless facts it promises and useless facts it gives, by the wagon-load! They're arranged in 18 different categories and if it's funny it must be true!

Lose Weight Instantly!

http://www.exploratorium.edu/ronh/weight

Diet not going well? Cheer yourself up by discovering how much less you'd weigh on Mercury, Venus, Mars, or any other planet in the solar system.

The Bureau of Missing Socks

http://www.funbureau.com

Find out more about one of the world's most frustrating mysteries. A brilliantly funny and much-needed site that includes a place where you can input details of your own 'single' socks, just in case the other one has been spotted somewhere in the world.

Uproar!

http://www.uproar.com

Play dozens of free games (some with prizes) at this fun-packed online game show.

Office Pranks

http://www.gwally.com/pranks/office

Liven up a boring day at work by trying out a few of the pranks listed here, from paging a bogus employee to taking a message for your colleague from Mr Bear (with the phone number of the local zoo!).

Thunk!

http://www.thunk.com

Apparently created for kids, this cute online machine will scramble messages for you – hours of fun for the easily amused!

The Anagram Server

http://www.anagramgenius.com/server.html

Type anything in the form and the Anagram Server will find, compute and display all the possible and, often hilarious, results. Hours of fun!

The Language of Sleep

http://www.sleepbest.com/habbit/frame-e.htm?/habbit/index-e.htm

Find out what your sleeping position reveals about your personality on this eye-opening (or closing) site.

Weird and Funny Stories

http://www.dysan.net/weird/weird.htm

The 25 shortest books ever written, 80 phrases that should be on buttons, the 11th commandment – these are just some of the short articles to be found at this amusing site.

The BoomBox Museum

http://www.pocketcalculatorshow.com/boombox

If iPods and mp3 players leave you cold, and you're strangely nostalgic for those old stereos designed to be carried on the shoulder, then this is the site for you.

The Marvels Of Toast

http://www.drtoast.com/recipes.html

Don't just put cheese or beans on it, use your imagination! Here you'll find some extraordinarily exotic recipes featuring, erm...toast.

Laugh Till You Cry

http://www.bigpuns.com

Groan over the latest puns from Punmaster Dan, or peruse past gems in the archives. No more, please, my sides are splitting!

Talk Like a Private Eye

http://www.miskatonic.org/slang.html

You can be talking like Sam Spade within a few seconds of visiting this site dedicated to PI slang. 'The two-bit flim-flammer jumped in the flivver and faded.' Exactly!

She's Mine Now

http://www.girlfriendstealer.com

It's not nice but it does happen, so get the lowdown here on girlfriend-stealing before it happens to you. Top tip: Apparently for both genders the number 55 on clothing is a sure sign of a stealer!

Interactive Underwear

http://www.interactiveunderwear.com

Send Frieda and Guido some underwear, and they'll wear it. If it's clean. They'll even take photographs of themselves to prove it.

Virtually Man's Best Friend

http://www.virtualdog.com

Perhaps you can't own a real dog due to restrictions of space or time... No problem, get yourself a virtual dog! You'll need to walk, exercise and train it of course… And you can compare how well your dog does with other dog owners!

Purity Tests Online

http://www.armory.com/tests

This 'Adults Only' site lists a large number of Purity Tests that can be found online. List what you get up to and get a 'purity rating'!

Clowns Are Evil

http://www.clownz.com

If big red noses and orange hair scare you, you must visit this site. Read about other people's experiences and explore the twisted world of childhood's worst nightmare...the clown!

One Potato, Two Potato...

http://www.readingtoes.com

Your toes may reveal more about you than you realize. Get the lowdown here from the official web site of the Foundation for Fundamental Dactylogical Reading. Yes, they are serious!

The Toilet Museum

http://www.toiletmuseum.com

'Ladies' Room', 'Men's Room', 'The Great Outdoors', 'Technotoilet' – just some of the toilet information to be found at this site. You can also sign the bathroom wall!

Retro Futures

http://www.retrofuture.com

Read what the pundits of the day expected life to be like in the 21st century (leisure 24/7, colonies in the sea, vacation trips to the moon), then ask yourself where it all went wrong.

'Build Your Own Cow' Page

http://members.tripod.com/~spows/cow.html

Add legs to the cow, heads, or even change the spots on this wacky page.

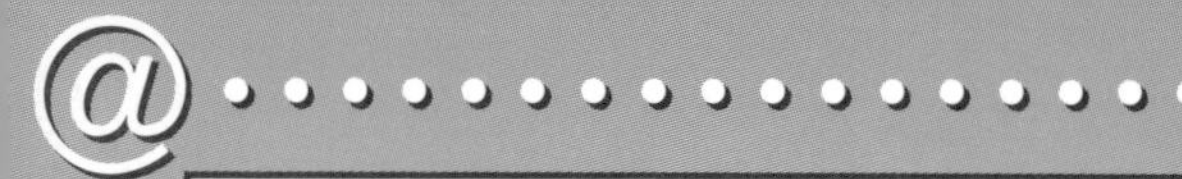

The Boring Page

http://www.cavaliers.org/john/boring.html

Fed up with smartass sites that take forever to load and crash your browser? Then pay a visit to 'The Boring Page', which is about as basic as a web site can get!

What Was That?

http://www.kissthisguy.com

Browse through the A–Z archive of hundreds of misheard lyrics, or join the fun and submit your own funny errors!

E-mail's Greatest Hits

http://www.bl.net/forwards

An extensive archive of those amusing and/or pointless e-mails that people forward to each other. Including such classics as 'M&M Duels', 'Prison versus Work' and 'Bedroom Golf'.

Ian's Shoelace Site

http://www.fieggen.com/shoelace/index.htm

Everything you never wanted to know about shoelaces, including how to tie the 'the world's fastest shoelace knot'!

Virtual Food Fight

http://www.virtualfoodfight.com

Start an e-mail food fight with friends or colleagues. Choose from a range of weapons, from spaghetti and meatballs to ice cream sundaes, then splatter away!

The Daily Message

http://www.dailymessage.com

This page offers you a wide range of choices that aim to brighten your inbox once a day, including e-mailed jokes, quotations, recipes, trivia and more.

Virtual Bubblewrap

http://www.urban75.com/mag/bubble.html

We have all done it, popped those bubbles – but isn't it disappointing when they are all popped? Well, here you can find virtual bubblewrap that you can pop forever!

Dog Years

http://www.patsyann.com/school/years.htm

This site makes calculation of the above very easy – you can sit and calculate the dog years of your entire family!

Bad Tattoos

http://www.badtattoos.com

Is that supposed to be a rose or an apple? Give your own ratings to some wince-inducingly bad tattoos. Look out for the 'Swiss Cheese' and the 'Clown With Guns' in particular.

Live Better, Live Cheaper

http://www.stretcher.com

Even if you think you're good with money, this page 'for professional tightwads' could be a real eye-opener. Read tips here about how to live better for less, and contribute your own.

A Gadzillion Things to Think About

http://www.geocities.com/Athens/Olympus/2843

With nearly 1,000 funny trivia questions to ponder, this site could entertain (or frustrate) you for hours!

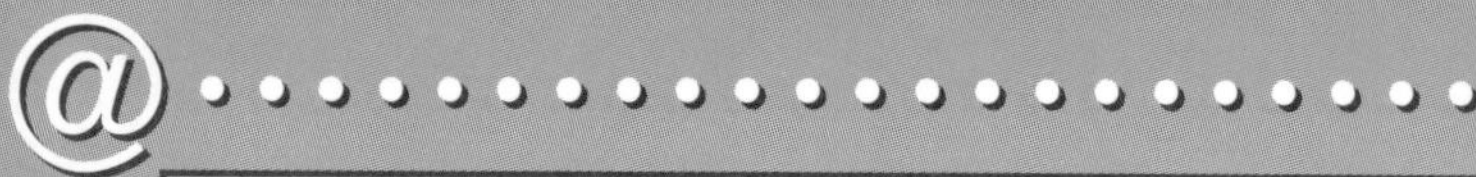

The Virtual Bachelor Pad

http://www.ziggyland.com

Visit the life of a bachelor! Peek inside the bachelor brain or tinker with the bachelor laundry system – if you dare!

The Gallery of Misused Quotation Marks

http://www.juvalamu.com/qmarks

A hilarious site with listings and commentary about 'quotation marks' that 'turn up' in the 'strangest' of 'places'.

Brain Flower

http://www.brainflower.com

Have you ever had a good idea to improve something? This page is full of hilarious and sometimes clever ideas submitted by people just like you!

Spirorama

http://www.spirorama.com

Do you remember that 1970s' toy, the Spirograph, which created fascinating spiral patterns based on mathematical principles? Well, now it's back and in full color on the Internet!

The Traffic Cone Appreciation Society

http://animation.filmtv.ucla.edu/students/awinfrey/coneindex.htm

Lying squashed and forgotten at the side of roads worldwide, this funny site felt there was a need to address the suffering of abandoned traffic cones.

The Perfect Present?

http://www.pileofmud.com

Looking for a gift for someone who has everything? This site also offers 'a range of absolutely dire presents', from the woodworm feeder to the teach yourself welly wanging kit.

Web of Lies

http://www.davesweboflies.com

There are nearly 4,000 lies at this site – for example, women are 12 times more radioactive than men! Unbelievable!

Y5B

http://www.Y5B.com

We've survived the Y2K bug – but will we survive the bugs when the clock rolls over into the year Five Billion AD? Prepare yourself for potential disaster by visiting this site.

The Crate Research and Application Project

http://vzone.virgin.net/sizzling.jalfrezi/slate/crate

You will simply never know how useful crates can be unless you go find out!

Doh!

http://www.dumbwarnings.com

Come here to read no-brainer warnings from businesses across the globe, e.g. the air conditioner that comes with the instruction: 'Caution: Avoid dropping air conditioners out of windows'.

Stupid Adverts From Finland

http://www.saunalahti.fi/~ivanoff/mainos

Who would have thought that the most stupid adverts in the world would come from Finland? View gems like: 'Your Cattle Is Waiting For Phosphate Fodder'.

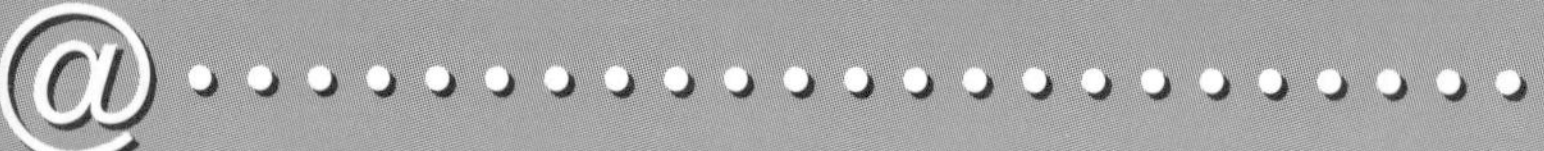

Computer Stupidities

http://rinkworks.com/stupid

Entertain yourself and feel strangely superior at the same time, as you discover just how stupid some computer users can be.

Find Your Star Wars Twin

http://www.outofservice.com/starwars

Via a short personality test, you can find out if you too are intimately related to a personality featured in Star Wars.

Pet Astrology

http://www.psychics.co.uk/petastrology/homepage.html

Pets have star signs too! This page offers you a horoscope reading for your own special animal.

Dancing Pillow

http://www.weebls-stuff.com/games/5/

There are hours of fun to be had causing the cute cartoon pillow to dance using only your mouse.

Facial Furniture

http://members.aol.com/antlavelle

How do you like your sideburns? Big and fluffy or sharp and sleek? This site is dedicated to this dubious facial apparel.

Cliché Finder

http://www.westegg.com/cliche

Need a cliché and need it fast? Over 3,300 cliches are listed and you can search them by keyword to discover (for example) how many include the word 'cat'. Why you would want to is another matter, of course.

Ultimate List Of Uses
http://www.eddnet.org.uk/comedy

Endless suggestions for how to make the seemingly useless useful. Examples include free ISP CDs (272 uses), Marmite (183 uses), and A Dead Cat (125 uses). The suggestions are rated from "nice and sensible" to "don't be so stupid" – with most tending toward the latter.

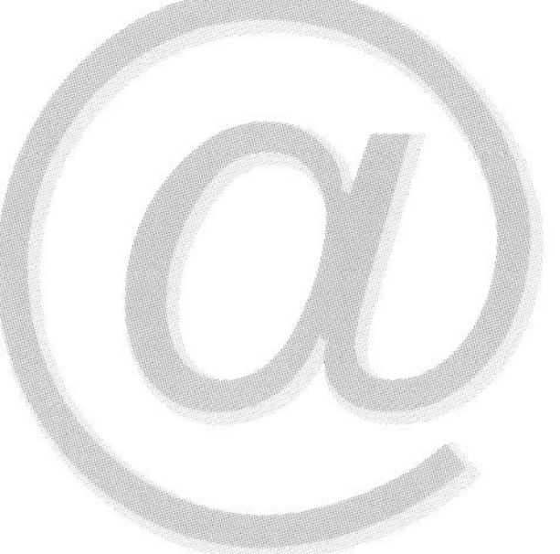

Angry Gingerbread Men

http://members.iconn.net/~phantom/ginger.htm

Have you got a killer Gingerbread Man tale to tell? Me neither. But plenty of people have... Pictures, stories, oh, and a recipe...

The Dilbert Zone

http://www.unitedmedia.com/comics/dilbert

Read Dilbert comic strips, watch an animated film or find out when he is next on television. You can even get a free Dilbert gift at this official site!

Dancing Paul

http://www.dancingpaul.com

Watch 'Cool Paul' dance to a selection of top disco tracks. You can even choose the scenery in the background!

Flip-book theater

http://www.bigempire.com/postittheater

Remember those mini-films we all made as kids by drawing a series of images in the corner of a notebook and flicking them over? Well, now they're live on the Internet!

The Life of a Hair Ball

http://mypage.direct.ca/k/kbotham/hairyindex.html

The photo-documented story of the life of a hair ball...the tragedy... the joy...and the drain!

Online Jigsaw Puzzles

http://jigzone.com

Click and drag the pieces to assemble these virtual jigsaws, from Michelangelo's David to Tulips in the Rain. Or you could just get a life instead.

Color It In

http://www.coloring.com

Re-live your childhood with the online coloring books at this site. There are over 100 pictures to choose from, with a new one added each week!

Trivia Heaven

http://www.funtrivia.com

The ultimate site for lovers of all kinds of trivia. Peruse the archives of subjects ranging from 'Animals' to 'Useless Trivia', enter the tournament, or try and answer the trivia question of the day.

Ghost Towns

http://www.ghosttowngallery.com

Are you fascinated by the images of ghost towns in old Western movies, with their abandoned buildings and drifting tumbleweed? Then this site is very definitely for you!

2

Gadgets, Gizmos and Novelties

How Are You Living Without One?

http://www.cycoactive.com/blender

You may have a television, a computer, a car, and lots of other really useful gadgets but do you have...a 'Blenderphone'?

Build Your Own Dalek

http://www.dalekcity.co.uk

Are you a Dr Who fan? Sign up here to learn how to make your very own 'Dalek', then sit back as your creations take over the universe for you...

The Lone Zone

http://www.lonezone.com

A solar-powered emergency radio, a pocket rocket massager, the Anti-gravity Handbook. A one-stop shop for bizarre and hard-to-find items, gadgets and books on the Internet. A must-see site.

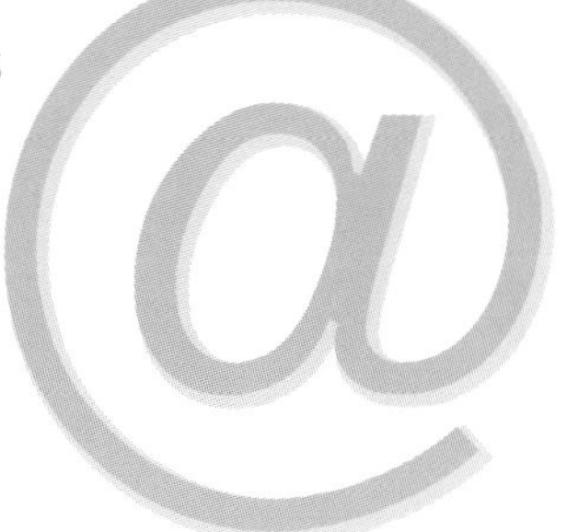

Revenge Is Sweet

http://www.revengeunlimited.com

Have you been wronged, mistreated, annoyed or ignored? Get your revenge here, with 'gifts' ranging from a box of melted chocolates to a bouquet of dead daisies!

Rubber Band Shooting

http://hometown.aol.com/morganbolt

Learn the fine points of rubber band shooting at this site. Your office colleagues will look at you with new respect!

Feeling Lucky Today?

http://www.7997.com

Where can you find a lucky horseshoe when you need one? This site offers worldwide delivery of authentic horseshoes in gold, chrome and copper.

Wacky Patent of the Month

http://colitz.com/site/wacky.htm

US Patent Number 2,139,001 is a 'Scalp-cooling Device'! Check out the other wacky patents and, for more serious advice, there are lots of links for inventors.

Who Wants To Be a Millionaire?

http://www.themilliondollar.com

Buy your very own million dollar bill for just $0.50.

Android World

http://www.androidworld.com

If making robots that look like humans, but don't complain when they are cleaning the house, is your thing – then this is a great site for you!

I'll Take It!

http://www.aso.com

Need a piston helicopter fast? How about a large transport jet? Visit this aircraft site to find out how much it'll cost you!

Go Gadget Go!

http://www.gadgetsontheweb.com

Divided into hand product sections, this innovative site has something for everyone, from flashlights to touch-screen calculators. Cool!

How Does It Work?

http://www.howstuffworks.com

Whether you want to know how chess computers work or what makes glass transparent, find out at this brilliant site hosted by the wonderfully named 'Marshall Brain'.

Bizarre Gifts for Your Pet

http://www.coolpetstuff.com

Does your pooch need an automatic water bowl? Perhaps you would like to strap him into his own motorbike seat. Wacky accessories for pets and humans alike.

My Pet Fat

http://www.mypetfat.com

A weight loss programme that involves carrying around a truly disgusting plastic replica of 1oz of body fat. If that doesn't work, try the 1lb or 5lb mypetfats!

Lawn Greetings

http://www.flamingosurprise.com/index.html

Surprise a loved one by covering their lawn with smiley faces, cows or teddy bears. Themed lawn ornaments for christenings, birthdays and other special occasions.

The Death Clock

http://www.deathclock.com

Plug your details into the 'Death Clock' and let it tell you how long you've got to go!

Kit Planes

http://www.kitplanes.com

Do you dream of having wings? Would you rather visit an airport than a movie theater? If you answered 'yes' to either of the above, then check out this site for lots of tips and info on building your own aircraft.

Bonsai Potato

http://www.bonsaipotato.com

Turn a humble potato into a fabulous sacred bonsai tree! The kit includes pruning shears, tweezers, and a replica altar for your spud.

The Museum of Modern Madness

http://www.madmartian.com

Twisted toward fake horror and science fiction, this site hosts the 'Plastic Eyeball Museum' and other such oddities.

Talking Toilet Paper

http://www.talkingtp.com

A toilet roll holder that plays a message when anyone pulls the paper. Record your own message, or use one from the manufacturer's extensive library of celebrity voices!

Totally Absurd Patents

http://www.totallyabsurd.com

A comprehensive look at the wackier side of inventions – with a huge number of related links and information. Check out the absurd patent of the week – when last checked the featured invention was 'Sleep-no-more Chin Balls'!

Movieprop.com

http://www.movieprop.com

For the low-down on the gadgetry, costumes and other props used in movie special effects, and how to become a collector, visit this fantastic web site.

AIBO – The Robotic Dog

http://www.aibo-europe.com

This incredible robotic dog has its own site, its own fan-club *and* its own magazine – check it out!

Infectious Disease Underwear

http://www.med-psych.net/doctor-gifts/novelty-gifts.html

A whole range of medical themed gifts and novelties, including underwear patterned with images of infectious diseases! Not to be worn on a first date.

Give the Gift of...?

http://www.nothing.net/nothing/index.html

What do you give the person who has everything? The answer is 'nothing'! This site has details about why 'nothing' makes a fabulous gift.

The Duct Tape Guys

http://www.ducttapeguys.com

We have all used it, we know how essential it is to life – but what else do we know about duct tape? This hilarious site offers you duct tape detail, fashion and history!

Uncle Booger's Bumper Dumper

http://www.bumperdumper.com

What is a 'Bumper Dumper'? Well...you could guess!...or you could visit this wacky site to find out!

Gobler Toys

http://www.goblertoys.com

A fantastic site that has to be seen to be believed – offering strange-looking and weird toys, both old and new.

Popular Science

http://www.popsci.com

For the gadget-geek who loves everything with wheels, wings, propellers or hard drives – this is the place for you! All the latest information about what technological marvel is being invented for civilians and the military alike.

Rube Goldberg's Annual Machine Contest

http://www.rube-goldberg.com

Inspired by the Pulitzer Prize-winning cartoonist Rube Goldberg, famous for his cartoons of wacky contraptions, this site offers the public a chance to enter their own wacky designs into an annual contest.

The Ultimate Gadget

http://www.victorinox.ch

How does anyone live without one? This is the official site of the Swiss Army Knife – it can do almost anything!

Weird and Wonderful Patents

http://www.lightlink.com/bbm/weird.html

A small but funny list of bizarre and utterly useless inventions including floating umbrellas and jet-propelled trains!

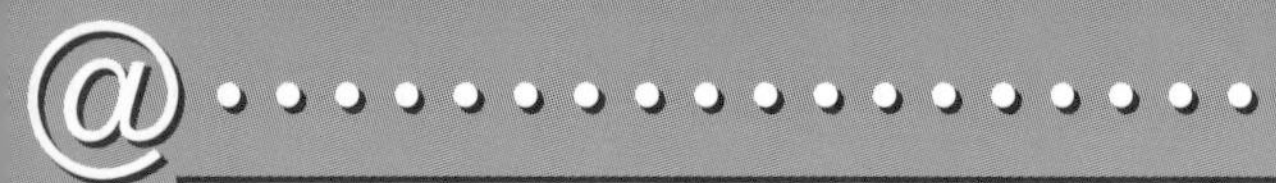

Thought Screen Helmet

http://www.stopabductions.com

Worried about being abducted by aliens? Help is at hand! This site takes you through how to build a useful thought screen helmet, step by step.

Unusual Gifts and Gadgets

http://www.rainbowsymphonystore.com

Anti-gravity toys, aquarium picture frames, unusual yo-yos, dolphin lamps, and a whole host of other gadgets that spin, shine, float and pulsate can be found here.

Gizmo City

http://www.gizmocity.com

An online store offering gizmos for the home and car such as 'Telephone Music-on-hold', a 'No-touch Light Switch' and a 'Wireless Mail Alert' (not for e-mail!)

Pretty Potty

http://www.funkytoiletseats.com

Use these fabulous novelty toilet seats to 'Bring Your Bathroom To Life'. An exotic range of toilet seats in weird and wonderful colours and shapes – including one that opens sideways!

The True Blue Roo Poo Company

http://www.roopooco.com

Paperweights and jewellery made from the authentic poo of kangaroos, koala bears and Tasmanian devils. Based in Australia, of course, but willing to ship worldwide!

Could You be a Zorbonaut?

http://www.zorb.com

Take one huge plastic ball, strap a person inside it, roll it down a steep hill...this is where you'll find out everything you ever wanted to know about the Zorb.

Solar-powered Bike

http://library.thinkquest.org/3684

Once upon a time, a group of students designed and built a solar-powered bicycle to enter a race. See how they did it and get lots of detail on the plans, construction and testing of this ultimate 'green' machine.

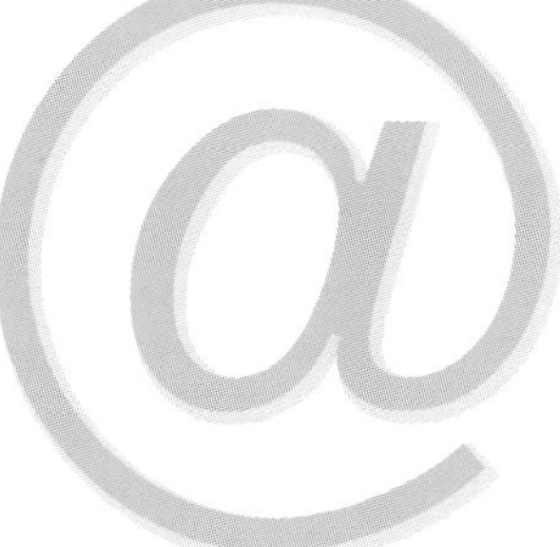

Hammacher Schlemmer

http://www.hammacher.com

The true home of strange and, sometimes, useful objects for sale, including gems such as 'Battery-heated Slippers', 'Backyard Dunk Tank', 'Carbon-monoxide-detector Alarm Clock' and an 'Artificial Sun'!

Useless Inventions

http://www.dailygadget.com/

Check out the very latest, most up-to-date gadgets, from the sleekest ipods to the weirdest banana bunkers.

Spook Tech

http://www.spooktech.com

Listening devices, night vision, covert spycams and tracking equipment are just a few of the items available at this online spy site.

The Obsolete Computer Museum

http://www.obsoletecomputermuseum.org

Where do computers go when they die? To this site! Check out the interesting exhibition pages.

The T-shirt Mall

http://www.tshirtmall.com

With categories such as 'Terrific and Outstanding Shirts', 'Internet Clothing' and 'Unusual and Bizarre' – this is a great place to find the perfect T-shirt for somebody you love or hate.

The Toilet-seat Lifter

http://www.thefactoryoutlet.com/toilet_seat_lifter.htm

This is the homepage for the 'Retrofitable Foot-activated Toilet-seat Lifter' – a one-of-a-kind!

Stupid Candy and Pasta

http://www.stupid.com

Computer-shaped pasta, severed finger candy – these and other odd delights can be found at this amusing web site.

The Unofficial Kinder Surprise

http://www.kindersurprise.org.uk

Come here to buy, sell or trade your Kinder eggs – or just trawl through the wealth of information about the extraordinary varieties of the little toys.

Shadow on Gadgets

http://www.spyshops.com

This site features the latest high-tech equipment for use as both 'security and private investigation tools' – they claim they will beat anybody's price on the Internet!

Bioresonant T-shirts

http://www.bioresonant.com

Don't wear dreary black - get some Bioresonant Harmony with these fabulous T-shirts, designed with colour healing in mind. The Bioresonant woven cotton shirts have the added advantage of making your arms happy too!

3D Glasses

http://www.3dglasses.net

Never be short of 3D glasses when you need them ever again! This great site has a huge range for you to choose from.

Party Poo-per

http://www.pooppals.com

Furry pets that poop jelly beans. Mmmmm. Hand-made in the US 'by only a handful of talented ladies', but ships internationally.

Neo-science

http://www.necrobones.com/neosci

This unusual site takes a look at the weird side of science – offering products and information on bizarre theories and scientific inventions.

The Robot Store

http://www.robotstore.com

Do you want to build a kit robot? This online store might be the place for you to start.

Spam Gifts

http://www.spamgift.com

Range of gifts relating to the famous and much loved canned meat from the Department 56 Spam Museum. Spam golf balls, spam 3D magnets and even a spam casserole dish! What more could you want?

The Chi Machine

http://www.chimachineusa.com

This strange health gadget claims to give you a 'Chi Rush' whilst it aligns your spine, improves your circulation and fixes your 'energy'.

How to Build Your Own PC

http://www.pcmech.com/byopc/index.htm

It really is easier than you might think. This site gives you fully detailed instructions on how to build your own computer...from scratch!

The Museum of Questionable Medical Devices

http://www.mtn.org/quack

A foot-powered breast enlarger, an electric machine to increase virility, soap that washes away the pounds – just a few of the wacky inventions that can be found at this fascinating site.

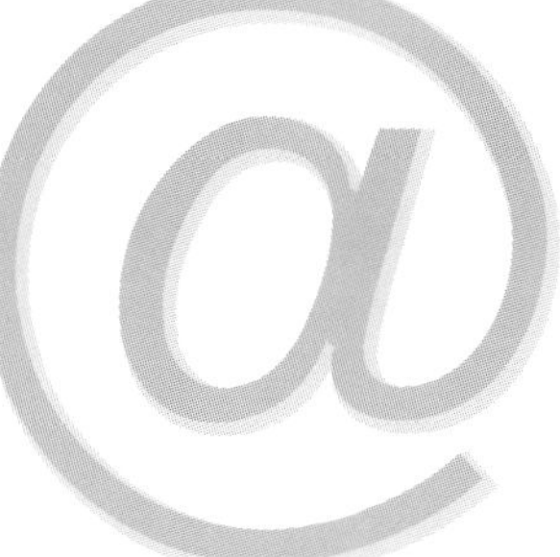

The Cauldron

http://www.thecauldron.com

Spell kits, statues, goblets and cauldrons are just a few of the 'spooky' accessories you can find at this mystical online store.

The 100 Greatest Comics

http://www.geocities.com/Area51/Aurora/2510/greatest_comics

Who are your favorite comic superheroes? This web site lovingly gives you the details of the top 100.

Caught Napping?

http://www.napping.com

Are you in need of napping information and snoozing accessories? If so, then this site was made just for you...if you can stay awake long enough to find it...(yawn).

Caution! Risqué Underwear!

http://www.cautionunderwear.com

A traffic-stopping range of underwear for men and woman, boasting slogans such as 'Toxic Fumes', 'No Entry' and 'Stop!'.

Home Improvement

http://www.diynet.com

A good general resource for advice, tips and connections to other home-improvement enthusiasts – the page for Mr or Mrs Fixit in your family.

Digital Typing Monkey

http://www.megalink.net/~ccs/monkey.htm

Can a virtual monkey randomly banging on a keyboard produce the complete works of Shakespeare? Log on here to find out!

Science Gear

http://www.amazing1.com/

This futuristic site features the ultimate modern 'devices' including High Energy Pulsers and Electronic Fishing Aids.

Gadget News

http://www.wired.com/news/gizmos

Get up-to-the minute news on the latest high-tech gadgets and gizmos (including some that don't work!) from the irreverent *Wired Magazine*.

Turtle Art

http://www.turtlekiss.com

Artworks by the world's only professional turtle artist, Koopa. You can buy Koopa's original artworks or commission something brand new. Koopa doesn't care. Koopa is a turtle.

Alien Abductions Inc.

http://www.alienabductions.com

Feeling left out in the abduction stakes? Wonder why aliens haven't picked you? This funny site offers 'genuine' abduction memory implants – out of this world!

See by Night

http://www.night-vision-goggles.com

Turn night into day with the range of night-vision binoculars, monoculars and goggles available from this site. Pretty cool.

Chindogu

http://www.chindogu.com

Chindogu means literally 'weird tool', and a growing range can be found here – from the backscratchers' T-shirt to duster-slippers for cats!

007 Gadget Lab

http://www.geocities.com/Hollywood/5727/q_lab.html

A brilliant site for descriptions of all the objects Q invented, including a snorkel attached to a seagull!

The Spy Tech Agency

http://www.spytechagency.com

Everything you need to become a spy – all the info and equipment, plus you can train with them from home!

Tattooed Clothing

http://64.225.33.220/default.asp

The realistic illusion of tattoos without any of the pain or commitment. Just pull on a 'tattoo shirt' and it will look as though your arms are covered with ornate tattoos.

Aquatic Bicycles

http://www.americanartifacts.com/smma/velo/velo.htm

If you always wanted to know about bicycles that could travel on or through water then this is the best place to look.

What's That Buzzing?

http://www.rctoys.com

On those rainy days when the TV just isn't enough – be the couch-pilot of a small flying airship. This nicely designed site also offers 'shiny, flying objects'!

Believe it or not!

http://www.amazon.com/exec/obidos/tg/detail/-/0439417678/103-7766513-7924629?v=glance

Robert Ripley explored more than 200 countries seeking all things bizarre and extraordinary. Buy this book packed with the weirdest, most outrageous inventions he could find! But only if you love the weirder side of gadget life.

Lawnmower racing

http://www.letsmow.com

Strange but true – people have been racing lawnmowers in the US and UK for over 30 years. Get the lowdown here on how you can turn a weekend chore into a competitive sport!

Dancetech

http://www.dancetech.com

Including user reviews and comments, this high-tech site gives you the latest in music hardware and mixers.

Veronica's Gadgets

http://www.veronica.co.uk

Serious music gear, such as transmitters and amps, can be found at this online broadcasting equipment store.

Celebrity Gear

**http://
www.heavenandearthandyou.com/**

Fancy owning a prop or gear that belonged to someone famous? Well, this is the place to purchase it!

Fly Power

http://www.flypower.com

Have you ever wondered if you could tap the energy of a fly to power a light aircraft? For details on how this is done and much more, visit this site. If you've never wondered and think it's a disgusting idea – there is a place on the site where you can voice your opinion.

3

Strange and Mysterious

In Search of Atlantis

http://flem-ath.com

A nice introduction site to the famous myth of the drowned city.

The Academy of Remote Viewing

http://www.probablefuture.com

If you want training in how to utilize mind technologies to 'view' locations in other parts of the world, or if you just want to read up about this conspiratorial technology, then this site is for you.

Feral Children

http://www.feralchildren.com/en/children.php

All about children who have been raised by animals: wolves, most commonly, although some have called gazelles, kangaroos and even bears, 'mom'.

The Jackalope Conspiracy

http://www.sudftw.com/jackcon.htm

The Jackalope is said to be one of the rarest animals in the world. But does it really exist? Visit this site for more information and a photo of the elusive creature.

The Supernatural World

http://www.thesupernaturalworld.co.uk

Vast, multi-award winning site looking at the supernatural, paranormal and unexplained phenomena. Particularly good for the mysterious creature 'Spring Heeled Jack'.

Fainting Goats

http://www-personal.umich.edu/~jimknapp/goats.html

Goats that faint? You must be kidding! But no, you can learn all about these rare goats at this site. Boo! Baa! Slump!

Strange News!

http://newsbop.triqi.com

A typical strange story on this site is, 'Owners baffled by globe-trotting pig', about a stone pig that one day vanished from its owner's garden and ever since then has been sending her postcards from around the world! Weird!

Spinetingling!

http://www.prairieghosts.com

Explore the haunted history of America with author Troy Taylor and the American Ghost Society.

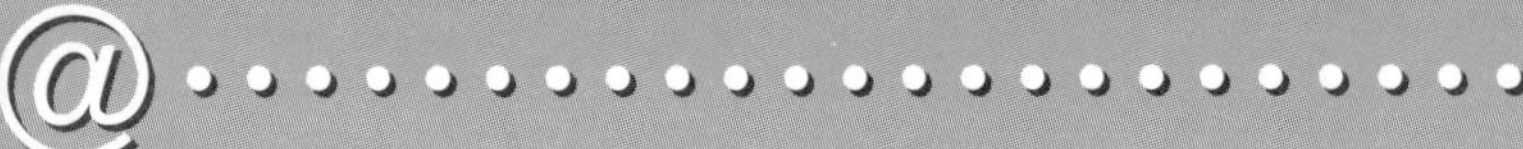

Voices on Tape

http://www.mdani.demon.co.uk/stunt/jun97s1.htm

This site is devoted to the mysterious 'spirit voices', which can sometimes be heard on tape recordings, even if no one was speaking at the time. Learn all about the phenomenon here.

Kirlian Photography

http://www.kirlian.org

A camera is offered on this site so that you can take your own 'aura' photographs – what color is yours?

Deathbed Visions and Out-of-body Experiences

http://www.healthsystem.virginia.edu/internet/personality/studies

The University of Virginia explores case studies on this web site – including out-of-body occurrences and children who claim to remember previous lives.

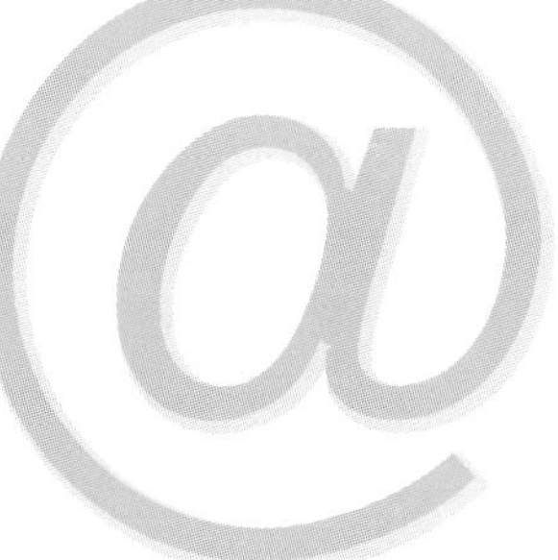

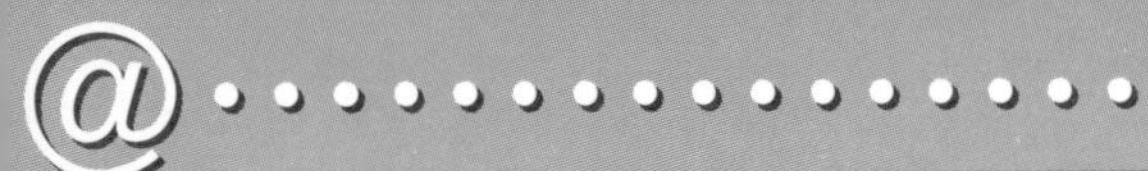

Parascope

http://www.parascope.com

Hot-off-the-press conspiracies.
A fascinating site with loads to read on current world events.

Haunted Places

http://www.haunted-places.com

This informative site lists haunted buildings and other places from all around the world. There's also a list of links to other good ghost sites.

Blow Your Mind

http://www.blowyourmind.net

If you have ever contemplated the history of medical miracles, time and space travel, parallel universes or the limits of reality, then this could be an interesting read for you.

Borley Rectory

http://www.borleyrectory.com

Get the lowdown here on 'Borley Rectory', said to be 'the most haunted house in England'. Spooky!

Haunted England and Ireland

http://www.afallon.com

Fancy staying overnight in a haunted castle in Ireland, or maybe a long weekend in one of England's haunted hotels? Check this site out.

Info Wars

http://www.infowars.com

Check out the news behind the news! This interesting web site has loads of articles and links about politics, religion and world events.

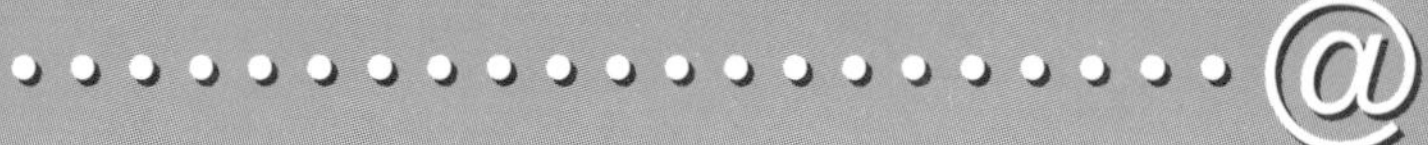

Reverse Speech

http://www.reversespeech.com

What are we *really* saying when we talk to someone? This fascinating site explains 'Reverse Speech Technology' and offers examples of famous people's speeches played backwards!

Mummy Is A Mummy Now

http://www.summum.org/mummification

Burial and cremation is all very well, but the classier way to enter the Afterlife is surely mummification? Treat yourself for around $67,000.

The Reptilian Agenda

http://www.davidicke.com

Ex-soccer goalkeeper turned conspiracy theorist David Icke's home page. Learn about the reptilian aliens' plans for us, see what you think of the future New World Order and much, much more.

The Skeptic's Dictionary

http://skepdic.com

For believers and non-believers alike, this site offers many fascinating, skeptical articles about a wide range of supernatural phenomena and myths.

Nostradamus Online

http://esoterism.com/nostradamus

This site offers the original writings of the famous predictor Nostradamus, as well as articles, news and other links.

Paranormal Search Engine

http://www.paraseek.com

This is a search engine and links site for the paranormal and unusual. Use it to search the web for paranormal sites, or read about real-life paranormal occurrences on the 'Investigations' page.

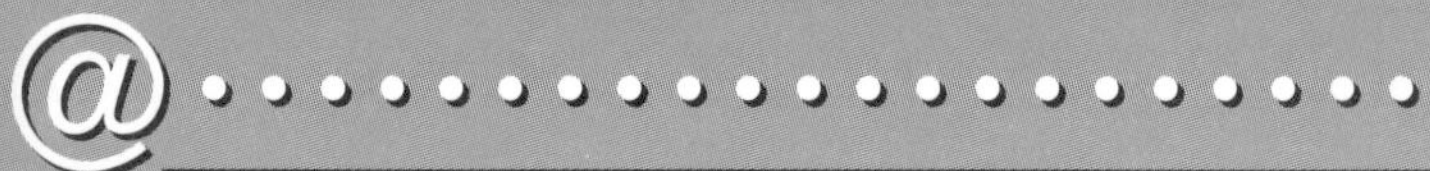

The Mystical Ball

http://www.mysticalball.com

Pick a number that corresponds to a shape, place your mouse over the mystical ball and the Virtual Wizard will tell you the shape you're thinking of. Telepathy or clever programming? You decide.

Near-death Experiences and the Afterlife

http://near-death.com

Visit this site to read about other people's experiences in near-death situations.

The End of the World – Not!

http://www.abhota.info

Fed up listening to the voices of doom and destruction? Cheer yourself up at this site by reading over 400 end-of-the-world predictions that failed to materialize, the earliest from 2800 BC!

Fortean Times

http://www.forteantimes.com

Unusual news site based on the magazine of the same name, featuring worldwide articles and eager to receive reports from people just like you!

Ghost Village

http://www.ghostvillage.com

Not so much a web site, more a community of folk interested in ghosts. There's even a 'Ghost Village' noticeboard, where you can post your supernatural photos and discuss orbs and ectoplasm!

The Museum Of Unnatural Mystery

http://www.unmuseum.mus.pa.us/unmain.htm

The exhibition halls of this online museum include Cryptozoology, UFOs and Weird Geology. Also includes an Ask The Curator feature. Spooky.

Demon Adoption

http://www.adoptademon.net

Not satisfied with a donkey or penguin? Now you can adopt a demon using this helpful site! Simply select the demon you wish to adopt, save it to your hard drive, register it and away you go!

Conspire

http://www.conspire.com

Visit 'Conspire' to see what's available to buy on the bookshelves under the heading 'Conspiracy'.

Yoga – The Cosmic Force

http://www.aetherius.org

This site helpfully explains the connection between the science of Yoga, the theology of all major religions and the mystery of UFOs. In case you had ever wondered...

Sacred Geometry

http://www.intent.com/sg

Find out on this fascinating site how the principles of geometry are reflected in nature. You can learn how the Nautilus shell uses a spiral generated by 'a recursive nest of Golden Triangles'!

Nessie Lives!

http://theshadowlands.net/serpent.htm

A rich site including amazing real-life photos and details of unknown sea creature sightings around the world. See it to believe it!

Sarah's Arch Angels

http://www.sarahsarchangels.com

Angel visions, angel pictures, angel rituals, angel poetry, and angel crafts and gifts. The whole angelic shebang.

Strange Magazine

http://www.strangemag.com

The online version of the off-line magazine of the same name - taking an objective look at strange and unusual phenomena.

The World of Unicorns

http://www.geocities.com/ Area51/Corridor/5177

This site offers art, quotes and links about the mythical one-horned horse – you can even adopt your own unicorn!

The Earth Files

http://www.earthfiles.com

A site devoted to strange environmental phenomena, including a good deal about crop circles. Includes the strange tale of 29,000 disappearing pelicans.

AIR Magazine

http://www.improb.com

This site deals with improbable research and calls itself the 'MAD Magazine of Science'. You can browse through the ezine online or subscribe to the off-line version.

Apocalypse Now?

http://www.mt.net/~watcher/new.html

This site is dedicated to theories and prophecies forecasting the end of the world, including conspiracies and information relating to the Bible and UFOs.

Computer-mediated Minds and Cyborg Bodies

http://www.island.net/~chrisbo

The melding of flesh and machine is a serious matter. This site has a large collection of articles concerning this modern computer-generated question – are we turning into cyborgs?

Crop Circles

http://www.cropcircleconnector.com /index2.html

All the very latest crop circle photos, news and links. If it's weird and it sprang up overnight, it's likely to be on this site!

The Werewolf Page

http://www.werewolfpage.com

Do werewolves really exist? Browse through the articles and case studies at this thought-provoking site to help you make up your mind.

Weird Encyclopedia

http://www.occultopedia.com/topics/creatures.htm

Whatever weird and wonderful topic you want to know about, from the Abominable Snowman to Zombies, the chances are you'll find it on this site.

Paranormal Radio

http://members.tripod.com/madmadmadworld/index.html

Log on here to hear Internet radio broadcasts from around the world on spooky subjects! Spooky!

World Mysteries

http://www.world-mysteries.com

Well-presented site dealing with lost civilizations, ancient ruins, sacred writings, unexplained artefacts, science mysteries and alternative theories.

Frightening Facts

http://www.ebaumsworld.com/ghosts.html

Mini documentary which covers ghost photography, ghost videos and electronic voice phenomena... complete with a funky, spooky soundtrack.

Dowsing

http://paranormal.about.com/cs/dowsing/

Dowsing the art of searching for hidden things (water, precious metals etc) using senses we're not even aware of! Learn more here.

The Telepathy Pages

http://www.spiritualists.org/telepathy.html

Find out about the method of mind-to-mind communication that parapsychologists call telepathy.

Dis-info-mation

http://www.disinfo.com

All sorts of conspiracy articles and theories about modern life, including articles from big names such as Robert Anton Wilson, are to be found on this fascinating and informative site.

The CIA – The Secret Team

http://www.ratical.com/ratville

An online book about America's foremost secret agency – if you are interested in political conspiracy theories, this is a must-read!

The FBI

http://foia.fbi.gov

Thanks to the Freedom of Information Act, you are now welcome to browse through the public reading room of the FBI – enjoy!

20/20 Vision for Peace

http://www.2020vision.org

A serious site dealing with environmental issues such as air pollution, toxins and over-population. Read the tips about grassroot activism or learn how to tap into the media for your cause.

Scientists and the Paranormal

http://www.issc-taste.org

An online magazine that delves into the strange and mysterious experiences of scientists. Their hope is that through the sharing of information we will better be able to understand the complexities of the human mind.

Astrology and Numerology

http://www.astrology-numerology.com

Learn about these twin mystic arts at this impressively detailed site. Use your new knowledge to help understand your true potential and decide the best times for major moves and activities in life.

In Search of the Giant Squid

http://seawifs.gsfc.nasa.gov/squid.html

Do these impressively large eight-legged monsters really exist? This might help you make up your mind!

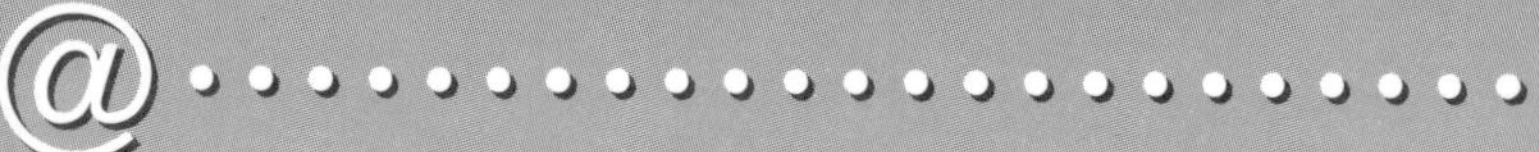

Stigmata Through the Ages

http://www.crystalinks.com/stigmata.html

This site briefly lists the famous stigmata cases in history.

The Psychic Investigator

http://psychicinvestigator.com

This nicely designed site puts the most popular paranormal events into a timeline. A good introduction to the most famous cases of our time, including those of Uri Geller and Harry Houdini.

Round in Circles

http://www.circlemakers.org

Crop circles – are they evidence of life from other worlds? This site dispels the myth and features a guide to creating your own.

Keys to Consciousness

http://www.themystic.org

Explore the mystical part of your life written by the 'internationally recognized master mystic', Graham V. Ledgerwood. Thirty-two life lessons in higher consciousness can be studied here.

Glossary Of The Paranormal

http://www.ufopsi.com/ufodc/glossary.html

More an encyclopaedia than a glossary, this site has a very comprehensive list of all the words, acronyms, study centres, key figures and places that relate to the paranormal and UFOs.

Lightning Strikes

http://www.disastercenter.com/lightng.htm

Everything to do with this powerful natural force...

Hauntings

http://www.ghosts.org

With a huge archive of stories collected from the Net and info on lots of specific haunting cases, this page is a must for anyone interested in ghouls.

Spooky 27...

http://www.lbstone.com/27

A conspiracy theory based around the number 27. A disturbing number of famous people including Kurt Cobain and Janis Joplin died aged 27, and this site probes further coincidences associated with the number.

Fixed Earth

http://www.fixedearth.com

If you thought money made the world go round, you're wrong – nothing does. It's fixed. Suspended between a couple of giant magnets. And it doesn't go round the sun either. That fool Copernicus led us all a merry dance.

The Atlantis Project

http://oceania.org

All about a new Atlantis – a floating city to be named Oceania. Plans are currently stalled, but who knows? There may yet be a flood of interest.

Chupacabra

http://www.elchupacabra.com/

Here are theories and info on the legendary goat-mutilating creature. Real or fake? You decide.

The Psi-dream Archive

http://members.aol.com/DreamPsi/archive

This fascinating site offers lots of info about shared dreaming and psychic dreams, and there's also an online mutual dreaming class that you can join.

Near-death Studies

http://www.iands.org

Read other people's accounts of near-death experiences, submit your own, browse the general info or even join the organization.

More Combustion

http://theshadowlands.net/mystery.htm

This site offers a summary of some reported and photographed cases of this nasty phenomenon – also includes some helpful links.

The Chinese Oracle

http://www.iching.com

The 'I Ching' is the Chinese oracle of changes, and on this site you can get a free reading. Just type a few words about your current situation or relationship, then click your mouse over the sacred pool to see what the stones reveal!

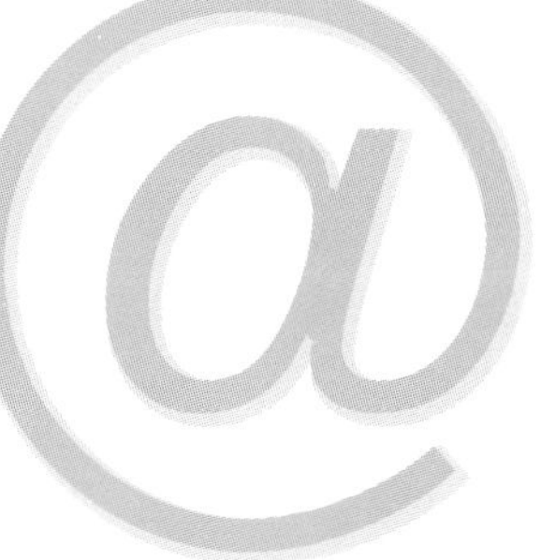

The Anomalist

http://www.anomalist.com

A fascinating online magazine dealing with scientific anomalies, unexplained mysteries and unexpected discoveries, such as vanishing hitchhikers and mass suicides.

Mystery Museum

http://209.150.104.203/

Doug Higley has amassed pictures of some very mysterious things indeed - freaks of nature or spawn of the devil - be prepared to be scared!

Planetary Mysteries

http://www.planetarymysteries.com

Claiming to be where 'science and art meet', this cool site features scientific facts and speculation.

Nessie's Grotto

http://www.simegen.com/writers/nessie

This is the nearest thing to a home page for the Loch Ness Monster. Read all about the legendary creature, including descriptions and photos of recent sightings.

Unexplained Mysteries

http://www.unexplained-mysteries.com

This site describes itself as the online interactive encyclopedia of the unexplained. Whatever you're interested in, find out all about it here.

PCP

http://pespmc1.vub.ac.be/Default.html

Attempting to 'tackle age-old philosophical questions with the help of the most recent cybernetic theories and technologies', this site includes memetics and ethics.

Sleep Paralysis

http://www.trionica.com

Often thought to be an alien abduction experience, a surprising number of people suffer from this torment. Visit to find out more!

The STATS Spotlight Archives

http://www.stats.org

An interesting web site that examines the true statistics behind government claims and news stories, including GM food production.

Bigfoot

http://www.bfro.net

Read through the theories and sighting reports, or pick up tips on tracking and collecting evidence at this site about the elusive big and hairy one.

The Shroud of Turin

http://www.shroud.com

The best place on the Net to go if you want more details on the famous shroud. Look at photos, read the articles and theories, then make up your own mind about its authenticity.

Wasting Time!

http://members.tripod.com/BabelOnline

Packed full of strange strangeness and bizarre facts, this kooky site has been wasting your time since 1995! Find out more!

Weird Mysteries

http://www.europa.com/edge/weird.html

This great site has it all – mysteries that are to be found on earth, in the air, in space, and even underground! You need never search again.

Strange But True

http://www.geocities.com/mikey_wbt/wbt.html

Mike Boyle has spent years assembling a massive collection of stories that in some way highlight the absurdities of human life. Now he's decided to publish it on the Internet. Read and be amazed!

Two by Two

http://www.arksearch.com/index.htm

You've watched Raiders of the Lost Ark, now read the true story and take a virtual tour of the Ark itself!

4

Far Out

Barf Bag Collection

http://sicksack.com

The largest, and possibly only collection of airline sick bags on the Net. Over 700 examples from 350 airlines. Swap sick bags with the site owner to form your own collection, if sick is your bag.

Dumb Crooks (aka Mentally Challenged Criminals)

http://www.dumbcrooks.com

Crooks aren't always the smartest people in the world. Visit this sidesplitting site to find out just how stupid they can actually be.

Sandcastle Central

http://www.unlitter.com/sandcastle/index.html

For serious sandcastle connoisseurs! Tips, news, contests and fascinating photographs of elaborate sandcastles.

Best in Show

http://www.worldbeardchampionships.com/index.html

The World Beard Championships are held every two years. But if you think your own beard is pretty handy and you want to enter, you'll face stiff competition – just check out some of the beauties here!

The Origins of the Universe Archive

http://www.talkorigins.org

This site explores the great 'Creation versus Evolution' debate and offers lots of background information for those who are new to the topic.

Purely Purple

http://www.purple.com

If you like the color purple, this is definitely the site for you. Just don't expect very much else!

The Weekly Onion

http://www.theonion.com

One of the Internet's best parody newspapers. This product is definitely worth browsing.

The Amazing 'Send Me a Dollar' Web Site

http://server.tt.net/send-me-a-dollar

It's amazing what people use the Internet for. Give this guy a medal! Check out how many dollars he has already accumulated – you won't believe it.

Floaty Pens

http://www.5th-sun.com/fpotw

Floaty pens are high-quality souvenir items that are sold worldwide; they're made in Denmark by the Eskeson Company. Marvel over the Buckingham Palace pen and the Graceland, then contact other collectors to trade yours!

Decimal Birthdays

http://www.jarusa.com/birthday/index.htm

Need an excuse for a party? Enter your birth date and this site will calculate your next decimal birthday. Now you can celebrate every 1,000 days of your life.

The Incredible World of Navel Fluff

http://www.feargod.net/fluff.html

How much belly button fluff do you think one person can collect in a jar in a year? This site claims to show you the record-holder. Useful, eh?

The Bad Fads Museum

http://www.badfads.com

Silly fashion, ridiculous sports and toe-curling past-times, plus much more from this site. Visit if only to remind yourself of the embarrassment you thought you'd left far, far behind.

The Museum Of Bad Art

http://www.museumofbadart.org

Are those ice creams or mountains? Countless examples of what happens when amateurs express themselves through the medium of paint.

Disco Fever

http://www.70disco.com

A web site entirely devoted to 1970s disco music. Profiles of bands, charts from the 1970s, and more!

Dean and Nigel

http://www.deanandnigel.co.uk

Dean and Nigel demonstrate how to blend in with ordinary members of the public. View their hilarious galleries, which show them 'blending in' with a range of bemused-looking people on Britain's streets!

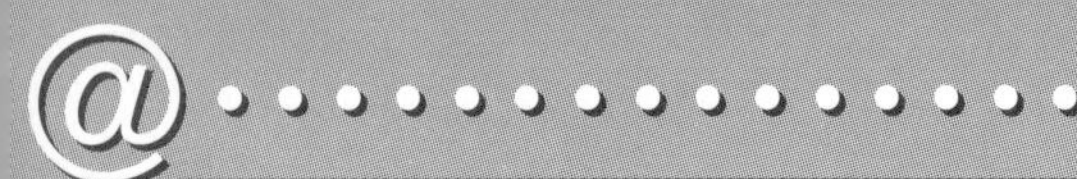

Ken White's Coin-flipping Page

http://shazam.econ.ubc.ca/ flip/index.html

Flip a coin and read the statistics on the coins already flipped – so just how many did come up heads anyway?

I Have the Bends!

http://www.contortionhomepage.com

Some people like to knit or fish in their spare time and some people like to do this! Ouch! Bet they always win 'Twister' though!

Fighting Ignorance

http://www.straightdope.com

'Fighting ignorance since 1973 (It's taking longer than we thought)'. Cecil answers all your strange and ignorant questions with quiet patience and cool reason. Is it true that elephants never forget? Why did Kamikaze pilots wear helmets? Find out here.

Dumb Laws

http://www.dumblaws.com

Taken from nations all around the world, this web site has archived laws that don't seem to make a whole lot of sense, for example, did you know that in Minnesota it is illegal to cross the state line with a duck on your head?

Toothpaste World

http://www.toothpasteworld.com

Have you ever tried to brush your teeth with chocolate? One man's collection of toothpastes from around the world. And more toothpaste-related fun.

Strange Finds

http://www.pavementgear.com

This site is dedicated to strange items found on the roadside, from Santa's hat to a pair of slacks with all the belt loops removed. We can only wonder how they got there!

How To Cope With Extreme Good Fortune

http://www.note.com/note/pp/jackpot.html

Straightforward, practical advice on what to do (and what not to do) when you win millions on the lottery.

The Cabbage Converter

http://www.geocities.com/ Heartland/Plains/2144

Have you ever thought to yourself, 'Gee, I wish I were a cabbage'? Well, now you can be! Check this site out to see how!

Modern Moist Towellette Collecting

http://members.aol.com/ MoistTwl/index.htm

Don't believe it? Check out the gallery for yourself – it features a whole array of damp little tissues!

'I Quit!'

http://www.iquit.org

Do you need some help e-mailing your boss? Do you want to see what has happened to others who have quit their jobs in ferocious moods? Visit this site to explore these questions and chat about your own lousy job!

And Adam Knew Eve

http://www.hobrad.com/and.htm

A comprehensive and amusing A–Z list of all the references to sex that can be found in the Bible.

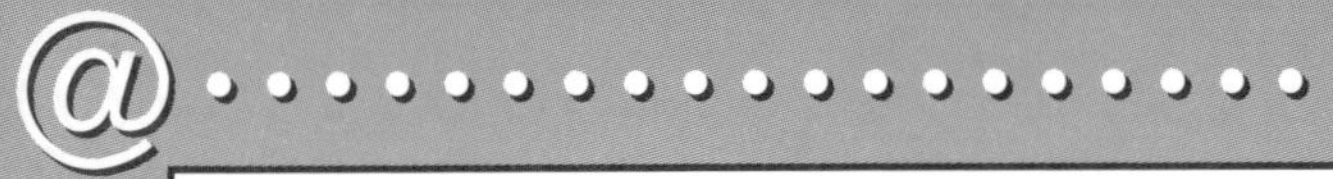

TV Eyes

http://www.tveyes.com

This incredible site offers to e-mail you when a word of your choosing is spoken on television – why don't you try it for yourself.

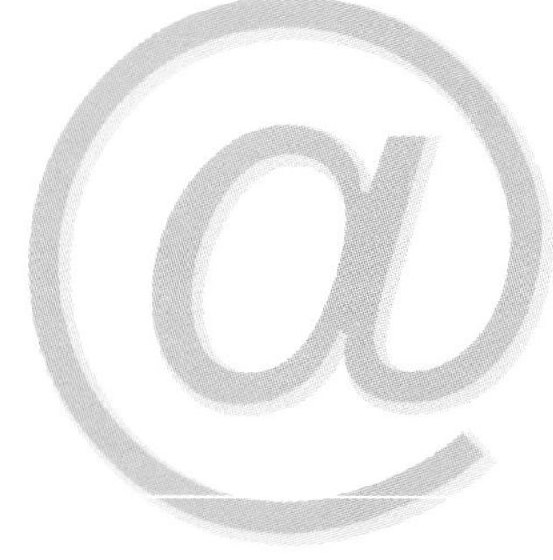

Gap-toothed

http://www.gap-toothed.com

A shrine to all those with gaps between their front teeth, including a gallery of photographs, articles and even a contest.

The Universe of Bagpipes

http://www.hotpipes.com

Everything you did and didn't want to know about bagpipes! The site includes an interactive gallery of various bagpipes that will play music if you ask them nicely!

Juggling Info

http://www.juggling.org

The only place to go if you are interested in juggling, including news, articles, links to juggling clubs and more.

Underground Animals

http://www.animalsontheunderground.com

The London Underground is full of escaped animals! First an elephant was spotted, then birds, cats, dogs… See if you can find a new species.

Earth-cam

http://www.earthcam.com

The huge number of 'cam' categories available on this page include science-cams, restaurant-cams, scenic-cams and religious-cams. Smile, you're on candid cam-era!

Brain Collection

http://brainmuseum.org

A comprehensive, if not a little unsettling, university collection of brains. Big ones, small ones, human and animal grey-matter are all on show at this site.

The Death Test

http://test.thespark.com/deathtest

Fill in the details and cringe, or alternatively celebrate, the results! How long have you got left?

Ultimate Taxi

http://www.ultimatetaxi.com

Why bother catching a cab to go to the local nightclub when the cab is the nightclub, complete with glitter ball and disco lights. Space is limited though – not for the John Travoltas of this world I fear!

The Latest Works

http://www.ritsumei.ac.jp/~akitaoka/saishin-e.html

A web site full of optical illusions designed to make your head spin. Examples include The Chameleon, Rotating Snakes and The Packed Cans. They really do appear to shift, spin and wobble.

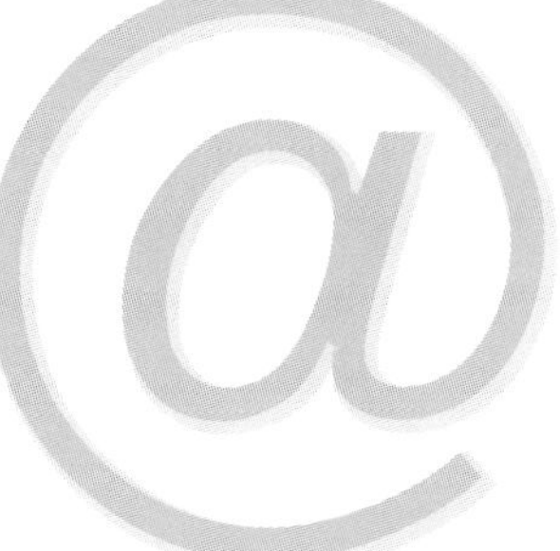

The Nose Page

http://www.well.com/ user/cynsa/nosepage.html

Add to the many photographs of noses already on the site by sending them a photo of your own hook, snub or ski-jump!

The Web-page Shredder

http://www.potatoland.org/shredder

The web 'shredder' lets you input an url of your choice – allowing you to become a web Picasso via unwanted web waste.

Reincarnation via Horoscopes

http://www.canuck.com/~akwu

Have you been reincarnated? This site thinks it can answer this controversial question – by reading your horoscope!

Roadside America

http://www.roadsideamerica.com/vortex.html

A guide to offbeat roadside attractions across the United States. Jamestown, ND has the world's largest buffalo of course, but the controversy over who has the world's largest chair rages on.

Restrooms Of The Future

http://www.restrooms.org

Did you know that 58% of men would like privacy partitions? Public restroom surveys, personal hygiene tips and other public toilet info.

Cooking By Numbers

www.cookingbynumbers.com

Just fill out the 'what's in your fridge?' and 'what's in your cupboard?' sections and the site does the rest – producing a list of possible recipes from the ingredients you have. Then get cooking!

Far Out

The Multicultural Web Recycler

http://recycler.plagiarist.org

This interesting site scrambles images from web-cams around the Internet and blends them into a work of art.

Mister Cyborg

http://www.cyborgname.com

Enter your name, choose a cyborg avatar, and get a whole new cyborg identity. If you like the sound of your cyborg name, you can use the graphic on your own web site or buy T-shirts and mugs with your new name printed on them.

Freespeling (with one "l")

http://www.freespeling.com

Apparently only 17% of native English speakers can spell properly, so this website campaigns to make certain English words easier to spell. You can vote for new spellings that you think would make life easier - like 'unconshus', 'garantee' and 'axident'.

Ask Doctor Toy

http://www.drtoy.com

Do you want to find out more about the most popular toys on the market? Doctor Toy is the best place to go for the low-down on little people (and big people!) and the gadgets that make them happy.

Eric Harshbarger's LEGO Pages

http://www.ericharshbarger.com/lego

Eric loves LEGO! See pictures here of some of his best creations, like the DNA double helix and life-size, functional grandfather clock!

The Language Kit

http://www.zompist.com/kit.html

JRR Tolkein did it. You can too! This is a very detailed guide to creating your very own language. Easy when you know how!

The White House

http://www.whitehouse.gov

The official site for the home of the US President. Handy if you want to keep your finger on the pulse of US politics – or if you want to send the President an e-mail!

Missile Base Road

http://www.missilebases.com

This site explores the concept of Missile Bases as 20th-century homes and has details of real bases for sale; have you got $300,000 spare?

The Payphone Project

http://sorabji.com/livewire/payphones

This web site invites you to submit a real payphone number from anywhere in the world. There is already a list of such numbers here – so make a call and see who answers!

Poor Fluffy!

http://george.lbl.gov/ITG.hm.pg.docs/dissect/info.html

This interactive site allows you to dissect a digital frog and there are links to serious info on frog biology.

Train Hopping Across America

http://catalog.com/hop

Need to get across America without much cash? Why not do it the old-fashioned way and hop the freight trains. This site has timetables, railroad maps and tips on how best to hop.

Transhumanism Resources

http://www.aleph.se

Transhumanism is about the future evolvement of human beings, including uploading human consciousness into computers, and life-extension techniques such as cryogenics. Visit this site for excellent information on a futuristic topic.

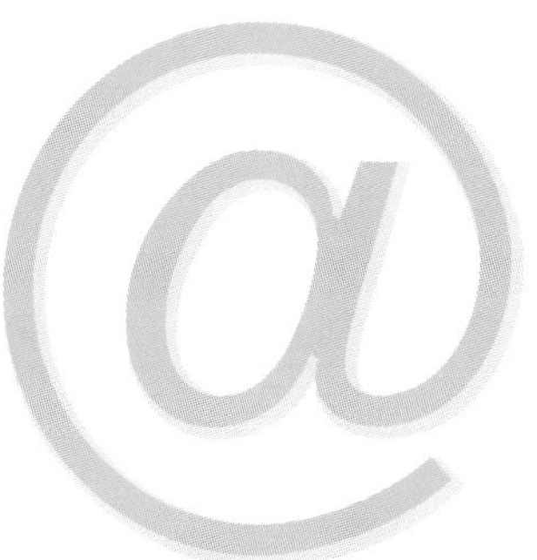

The Scary Baby Conspiracy

http://www.scarybaby.com/babyoftheweek.html

Perhaps you have your own scary photos of a family baby? Check out this funny site for 'scary baby of the week'.

I Love Cheese

http://www.ilovecheese.com

A lot of people like cheese, but how many really love it? Enough to eat a Wisconsin Aged Cheddar Cheese Ice Cream? Guides, recipes and links for the total cheese fanatic.

Sea Monkeys

http://www.seamonkeyworship.com

If you can't remember these, then visit this site for everything you could ever want to know about these strange creatures.

Virtual Message In A Bottle

http://www.hoosiertimes.com/cgi-bin/bottle

Send a virtual message in a bottle, and it will arrive on the shore of someone else who's sent a message...and who knows where it'll all lead?

Sodaplay Zoo

http://www.sodaplay.com/constructor/index.htm

Create and animate your own imaginary creatures here, then place them in the 'Sodaplay Virtual Zoo' for others to admire!

Surfing Sobriety Test

http://www.turnpike.net/~mirsky/drunk/test1.html

Are you sober enough to be surfing the net? Take this test to find out. Hope you don't see double!

Paper Dolls

http://www.opdag.com

Including tips on how to get your paper dolls published and their history – this is the only place to come for all the info on...yes!...paper dolls!

Plane Sailing

http://www.paperairplanes.co.uk

Most people content themselves with the standard 'dart' model, but if you want a paper plane that out-flies all the rest, here's the low-down on the origami required.

The World Federation of the Right to Die Societies

http://www.finalexit.org/world.fed.html

As the title suggests, this site is dedicated to the intensely serious subject of euthanasia. It offers lots of information about the laws of different countries and tries to answer some difficult questions.

The Picasso Conspiracy

http://web.org.uk/picasso

An extensive site concerning the discovery and suppression of Picasso's 'Unknown Masterpiece', a secret work from 1934, full of occult imagery.

Everything Ideas

http://www.everythingideas.com

Ever had a great idea that you really wanted to share? Here's a site that's full of brilliant ideas submitted by surfers. Examples include clear shoes, and getting rid of the letter 'A' to make typing faster (fster).

Warning!

http://www.aviationpics.de

Ho-hum! One minute you are sitting on the beach enjoying the sunshine and minding your own business, the next, an aircraft skims the top of your head! Don't believe me?

Incredible Stuff I Made

http://www.cockeyed.com/incredible/incredible.html

Rob's page of incredible stuff he's made from frankly very limited resources. A banana skin coat, for example. And a cat coffin.

Bork, Bork, Bork!

http://www.rinkworks.com/dialect

Featuring 'The Dialectizer', this funny site allows you to change your dialect! Now you too can sound like a character from The Muppet Show!

Eric's Emotions

http://www.emotioneric.com

Request an emotion at this site and Eric will do his best to act it out for you. There is already a fantastically long list to choose from!

Poison Ivy Rash Hall Of Fame

http://www.poison-ivy.org/rash/index.htm

A gallery of submitted pictures showing the perils of coming into contact with poison ivy. Some of the pictures are truly disgusting, but if you've ever had a poison ivy incident yourself, here's where to share your pain.

Don't Give a Fig?

http://www.godhatesfigs.com

If you do too, you can join in their write-in campaign and read terrifying fig-related disaster stories.

The Bureau of Atomic Tourism

http://www.atomictourist.com

Do you fancy a trip to a nuclear test site? Or perhaps you would rather visit a place where the bombs are actually made? This site gives you the low-down on all things atomic!

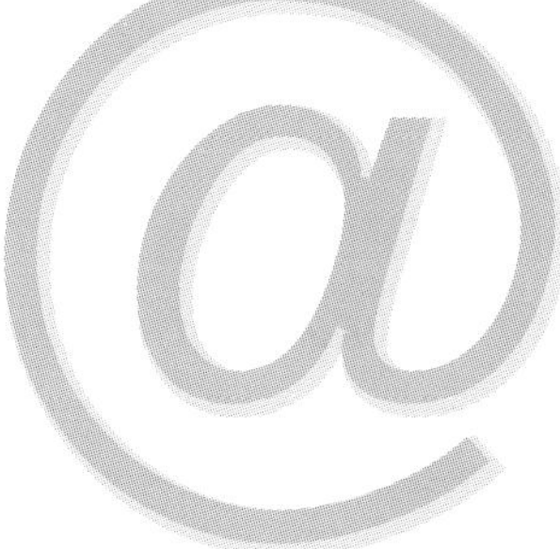

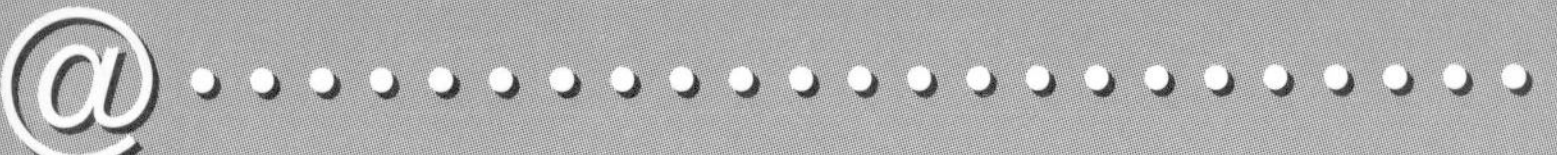

Weird Virology

http://www.virology.net/WeirdVirology.html

This web site takes a look at some of the biggest diseases threatening us and some of the weird 'cures' on offer.

The Darwin Awards

http://www.darwinawards.com

Responsible for 'commemorating the remains of individuals who contributed to the improvement of our gene pool by killing themselves in really stupid ways'.

Circus Trees

http://www.bonfantegardens.com/trees/treesa.html

View pictures of wonders woven from living wood, creating trees in the shape of hearts, lightning bolts and rings.

The Dark Side of Scooby Doo

http://www.cdc.net/~drjekyll/scooby/darkside

Finally someone has seen through the disguise – visit this site to view the alter egos of Scooby, Scrappy, Velma, Freddy and Daphne.

The Dull Men's Club

http://www.dullmen.com

There had to be a place on the Internet for dull men – and here it is! Marvel at what the 'dullest of dull' men do in their spare time.

Klingon

http://www.kli.org

Some people take television very seriously. Visit this hilarious site to find out everything a Trekkie would want to know about Klingonese!

Regia Anglopum

http://www.regia.org

If you would like to dress up as a Viking every weekend, then this is the place to come...

Take a Drive

http://www.webtruck.org/webtruck

Jump on board and take the toy truck for a spin. You can go backwards and forwards, load and unload marbles, and see the view from the on-board camera. Good, clean interactive fun!

Shake It Hammy!

http://www.hamsterdance.com

They are all here – dancing aliens, lizards, cows and even armadillos! Dance the night away with them in style!

Mind Your Head!

http://www.dartbase.com

Darts is a serious business – not just an old British pub game. Read the tips and improve your throw at this sharp site.

5

Celebrity Weirdness

Jerry Springer World

http://www.uni-television.com/jerry/theshow.html

You know you want to! Visit the official site of the Springer show to find out all about the wacky show topics and the man himself – you can even send him an e-mail!

Celebrity Astrology

http://www.metamaze.com/mmWL.html

When you just have to find out what sun sign Tom Cruise is, or Pamela Anderson, or Brad Pitt, or...

Famous Heights

http://www.famousheights.com

Do you lie awake at night wondering how tall your favorite celebrity is in real life? If so, you should definitely stop by this site.

Famous Quotations

http://www.famous-quotations.com

Check out the most interesting, funny and profound quotations from famous people throughout history. Guess who said, 'A jury consists of 12 persons chosen to decide who has the better lawyer'.

Celebrity Belly Buttons

http://www.megspace.com/entertainment/famousnavels

Forget their acting skills – do they have an "inny" or an "outy"?

Former Child Star Central

http://members.tripod.com/~former_child_star/index.html

Visit this site to find out just what happened to those cute and not-so-cute kids who used to be famous on TV and in the movies. Whatever happened to Macauley Culkin?

Return of the Muppets

http://www.muppets.com

TV's top puppets review their favorite web sites. There's games galore and you can find out what Miss Piggy is up to at the moment!

Skinema – Dermatology in the Movies

http://www.skinema.com

A funny site with a serious message... here you can find lots of details about how *not* to look after your skin.

Men Who Look Like Kenny Rogers.

http://www.menwholooklikekennyrogers.com

After a certain age, a lot of men start to look like Kenny Rogers. So many that this site has had to close to new submissions. But there's almost 1,000 photos in the picture gallery, a guide on How To Look Like Kenny and, um, a corn muffin recipe.

Celebrities Exposed

http://celebrities.fun.ms/

See how the famous look when they aren't expecting a photo shoot!

Houses of the Rich and Famous

http://www.latimes.com/classified/realestate

Would you like to own a celebrity mansion? This is where you will find market details on which stars are selling their homes and how much you will have to save to buy it!

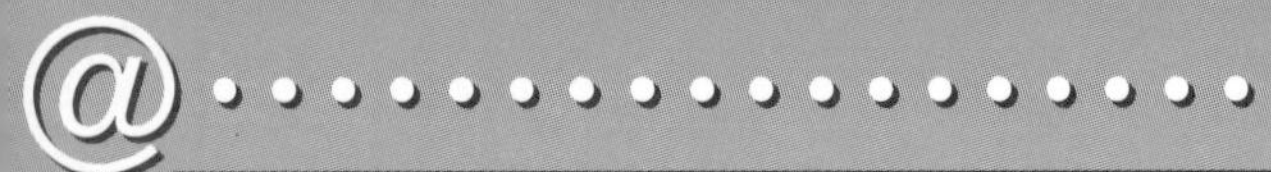

Court TV Online

http://www.courttv.com/trials/famous

Read all about world-famous court cases, past and present, on this site run by America's Court TV station.

Last Words

http://www.geocities.com/Athens/Acropolis/6537

Find out what presidents, philosophers, writers and famous business people had to say on their deathbeds!

Celebrity Site of the Day

http://www.csotd.com

A different celebrity site is listed every day here, and you can also see an archive going back to 1996. Your favorite celeb is sure to be here somewhere!

Celebrity Palace

http://www.celebritypalace.com

Come here for biographies, photos and fun facts on a wide range of celebrities, plus links to other celebrity web sites.

Who?

http://www.who2.com

A search page for famous people – this site provides links to fan sites, official sites and other useful information about the stars we love to love.

Nobel Peace Prize Winners

http://www.almaz.com/nobel

Covering the categories of literature, physics, chemistry, peace, economics, physiology and medicine – this is your chance to find out all about the Nobel laureates of our time.

Showbiz news!

http://movies.go.com

One of the best sites on the Net to find out what's hot and what's not in the world of movies and music. Check out your favorite celebrity or just read the news and gossip!

The Dead Musician Directory

http://elvispelvis.com/fullerup.htm

'A site about dead musicians...and how they got that way'. You can search by name or by cause of death, and there's even a latest late musicians section.

Star Spotting in Hollywood

http://www.seeing-stars.com

Everything you've ever wanted to know about where the stars play, work and live. Also find out about famous Hollywood landmarks and streets.

Arched Eyebrows

http://www.eyebrowz.com

This site offers do-it-yourself templates so that you can recreate the furry but feminine arches of stars such as Demi Moore, Gillian Anderson, Ingrid Bergman and Helena Bonham-Carter.

Celebrity Collectables

http://www.celebritycollectables.com

Authentic last wills and testaments, divorce files and autopsy files relating to your favorite celebrities.

Celebrity Screensavers and Wallpaper

http://www.celebrity-wallpaper.com

Just what you've always wanted – a picture of your favorite star that you can download and install on your computer screen. You need never miss them again!

Famous Birthdays

http://www.famousbirthdays.com

Find out which famous people were born on the same day as you...you might be surprised!

Celebrity Baby Names

http://www.celebnames.8m.com

Look up your favorite celebrities at this site and find out what exotic, strange and, sometimes, ridiculous names they give to their offspring. Who do you think would name their three daughters Rumer, Scout and Tallulah?

Celebrity Death Pools

http://stiffs.com

A twisted but amusing site that lets you dabble in a little virtual gambling. Who do you think will push up the daisies next?

The Celebrity Café

http://www.thecelebritycafe.com

This online magazine features celebrity interviews, music reviews, travel stories, and more. There's loads to see here!

E-mail Santa

http://www.santaclaus.com

All-year-round e-mail access to the jolly, red-suited man himself.

New Line Cinema Auction

http://www.newline.com/nlcauction/upcoming/

Newline Films regularly auction off costumes and props from their latest films – here's your chance to own Austin Powers' suit or Freddy Krueger's Leather Blade Glove.

The Internet Movie Database

http://us.imdb.com

A huge site offering movie news, information and reviews. Your one-stop shop for everything movie-related.

Famous Mug-Shots

http://www.mugshots.org

Sometimes they just can't help themselves and end up behind bars! This small but entertaining site shows you the actual prison mugshots of some small and many big names.

Celebrity Love

http://www.celebmatch.com

Ever wanted to know how compatible you are with Britney Spears or Brad Pitt? Or wanted to know which celebrity is your true love match? CelebMatch uses the 'scientific' method of biorhythms to calculate your ideal celeb love.

Hollywood Gossip and Chat

http://www.jtj.net/jtj/gossip.shtml

This site hosts various online chat rooms to gossip about the stars. Some say that the stars will even gossip back to you!

Who's Alive – Who's Dead?

http://www.neosoft.com/~davo/livedead

Covering actors, musicians, athletes, politicians and more – this site gives the real low-down on who is still breathing and who isn't. A good site for settling arguments between friends!

The Obsessive Fan Sites Reviewed

http://www.ggower.com/fans

This site tracks down obsessive fan sites for different celebrities and gives awards for the most extreme and ridiculous.

The Celebrity Almanac

http://celebrityalmanac.com

If you really want to know what's happening in celebrity-land, this cool site is definitely the place to come. It's packed with fascinating information – for example, did you know that Cheryl Ladd's real name is Cheryl Stoppelmoor?

Find a Celebrity Site

http://www.celebrity-link.com

Want to find web sites dedicated to your favorite celeb? The searchable database on this site contains over 5,600 celebrities and has a total of more than 22,000 links.

Celebrity Golf

http://www.celebritygolf.com

You'd be surprised who enjoys a round of golf. Alice Cooper for example. Exclusive interviews and links to other sites featuring celebrities and golf.

Famous Left-handers

http://www.indiana.edu/~primate/left.html

Included in this site are details of left-handed artists, actors, musicians, athletes and US Presidents.

The Millionaire Magazine

http://www.millionaire.com

Containing real information aimed at real millionaires, this online magazine charts the fortunes of the richest amongst us and features luxury goods and even an auction.

Celebrity Recipes

http://www.recipegoldmine.com/celeb/celeb.html

If you fancy nibbling Katharine Hepburn's brownies, swallowing Nixon's meatloaf or getting your hands on William Shatner's muffins, here's your site!

Celebrity Death Match

http://www.mtv.com/onair/deathmatch

The homepage of the television series of the same name. Come to this site to see the two Mansons or the Spice Girls battle it out in the ring.

The TV Single Dad's Hall of Fame

http://www.tvdads.com

They are a small but worthy minority, coping courageously with kids, dogs, and their own love lives. They are...single dads on TV.

Entertainment Online

http://www.eonline.com

The homepage of entertainment, featuring gossip, news, links to celebrities and much more. A good place to start a search.

Oprah Online

http://www.oprah.com

The queen of chat shows has her own web site! There's fun details on the show itself and also links to self-help articles.

The Celebrity Zone

http://www.celebrityzone.co.uk

This site provides photographs and information on all your favorite celebrities. Included are movie stars, pop stars, models, sports stars and TV stars. Test your celebrity knowledge with the quiz.

The National Enquirer Online

http://www.nationalenquirer.com

The *National Enquirer* is one of America's leading celebrity tabloids. Visit to find out the latest gossip on a star near you.

The Right Royal Family

http://www.royal.gov.uk

This is the official site of the British monarchy – not too much gossip available here but an excellent all-round resource for information, including photos and the history of the royals.

Hollywood.com

http://www.hollywood.com

The name says it all. This is a huge site and search engine for all things Hollywood. If you are looking for news or gossip, you'll definitely find it here.

Celebrity Games

http://www.celebritygame.com

Want to play a game with your favorite celebrity? Well, now you can! This cool site has free online jigsaw puzzles and other games featuring the celebrities of your choice!

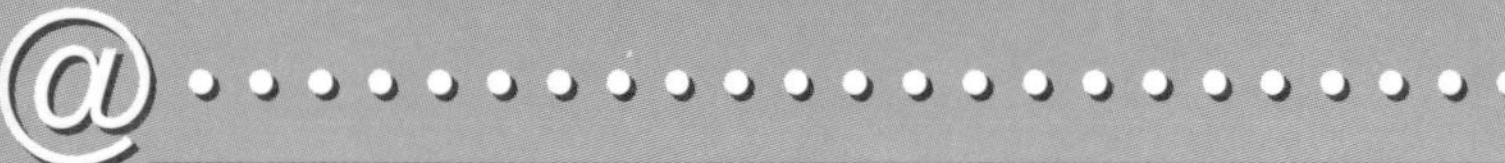

Chic Happens

http://www.hintmag.com

Who wears what and where? The inside gossip on celebrity fashion.

Annoying Celebs

http://www.newgrounds.com/assassin/

Are you sick of sycophantic celebrity sites? Then if you fancy virtually assassinatinating a star then release that aggression and go for it - but it's all legal and online only.

Mad Monarchs, Terrible Tsars, Crazy Caesars and Deranged Dukes

http://www.xs4all.nl/~kvenjb/madmon.htm

This site contains short, yet fascinating, biographies of mad members of the ruling classes in different parts of the world and throughout history.

Great Women

http://www.greatwomen.org

The National Women's Hall of Fame seeks to honor women of achievement. Search their growing database of high-flying females, or nominate a new entry yourself.

I Wanna Be Famous

http://www.iwannabefamous.com

Making ordinary people famous one person at a time. Submit a photo and profile and get your 15 minutes of fame.

Quote – Unquote

http://fly.to/quoteunquote

Here you'll find quotes from celebrities on a variety of subjects. Who do you think admitted 'In the gym, I only wear black and diamonds'?

Time Magazine's Top 100

http://www.pathfinder.com/time/time100/index.html

We all have an opinion on the most influential figures of the 20th century – find out who *Time Magazine* voted for.

Warp Factor

http://www.allfunnypictures.com/warp.html

Be it george Bush or Hugh Grant, take a face, move your mouse and warp them to your heart's content.

Pop-culture Junk Mail

http://www.popculturejunkmail.com

This site offers links to pop culture-themed web sites with a bias towards British royalty, movies, the 1980s and much more.

The Weird Site

http://www.theweirdsite.com/

There's weird news, weird facts and weird freebies on this site. Check it out!

The Fame Tracker Almanac

http://www.fametracker.com

A cornucopia of gossip, tidbits and news. A stylish site that tracks the movements of the stars so you don't have to.

Celebrity Stock Exchange

http://www.bbc.co.uk/celebdaq

Use your skill and judgement to buy and sell 'shares' in celebrities. Every week the shares you own will pay out a dividend depending on how much press coverage your celebs receive!

Search a Celeb

http://www.celebhoo.com

A search engine for finding out everything about the celebrity of your choice. A good place to start in your hunt for trivia, gossip or celebrity news.

Pitt of Horror

http://www.pittofhorror.com

Let horror movie legend, Ingrid Pitt, tell you all about the latest horror happenings and news from around the world. Oh, and you can join her spooky fan club too!

Famous Vegetarians

http://www.famousveggie.com

Find out which of the rich and famous don't eat meat. You can also browse recipes and find out how to make vegan chocolate pudding.

Make His Day

http://www.clinteastwood.net

Loads of top Clint Eastwood stuff here. You can even download a message for your telephone answering machine!

Biographical Dictionary

http://www.s9.com/biography

This is a searchable site containing a gigantic database of notable men and women who have shaped our world, from ancient times to the present.

Who Would You Kill?

http://www.whowouldyoukill.com

This irreverent and funny site runs several polls asking which character you'd kill off from various TV programs. The resulting statistics are as follows...

Pope John Paul II

http://www.vatican.va

No, you're not mistaken – the Pope is online! This is his official web site where you can read articles and find out about papal blessings.

Celebrity Diaries

http://www.diarist.net/links/celebritydiaries.shtml

Celebrity diaries and biogs from the likes of Anna Kournikova, William Shatner and Ian McKellen.

Famous Cats and Dogs

http://www.citizenlunchbox.com/famous/animals.html

Can't think of that cartoon cat you used to love? Need some naming ideas for your pets? This is the place to come.

This Movie Sucks!

http://www.mrcranky.com

Mr Cranky always finds reasons to object to the latest movie releases. You won't believe what he gets away with!

Hair Today, Gone Tomorrow

http://www.hairboutique.com/JerkyFlea/JerkyFlea.htm

Despite lots of time and money, even celebs have bad hair days! Log on to Jerky Flea's wicked commentary on the latest hair disasters of the rich and famous.

Rubber Faces

http://www.rubberfaces.com

Have fun playing with celebrity 'rubber' faces! Give them giant foreheads, fat lips and strange eyes. Over 80 celebrity faces to choose from, including Bill Gates, Sarah Michelle Geller and Michael J Fox. And a gallery with some of the highlights.

Canadian Celebrities

http://www.canadiancelebs.com

Browse through the biographies of Canada's leading actors, comedians, sportsmen/women, amongst many other professions!

Write for Hollywood

http://www.scriptsales.com

Got an idea for the next big blockbuster movie? Check out this site for all the latest scriptwriting advice and gossip. Now, all you need is for Tom Cruise and Jennifer Aniston to come on board...

A Celeb on Your Desktop

http://www.celebritydesktop.com

Do you have a favorite celebrity? Then why not install him or her on your computer permanently as a screensaver or wallpaper? There are thousands of free downloads here, from Angelina Jolie to Michael Jackson!

Film Flaws

http://www.moviecliches.com

Listed by topic, this fab web site contains the most common and annoying celluloid clichés.

Celebrity Horoscopes

http://www.demon.co.uk/kdm/celeb1.html

View the birth charts of a range of celebrities, with detailed astrological interpretations. Lots of juicy gossip here!

Barefoot Celebrities!

http://members.tripod.com/~a_spring/barefoot2.html

This little site is devoted to the bare feet of the rich and famous, from Tori Amos to Jon Bon Jovi. Just be grateful you can't smell them too!

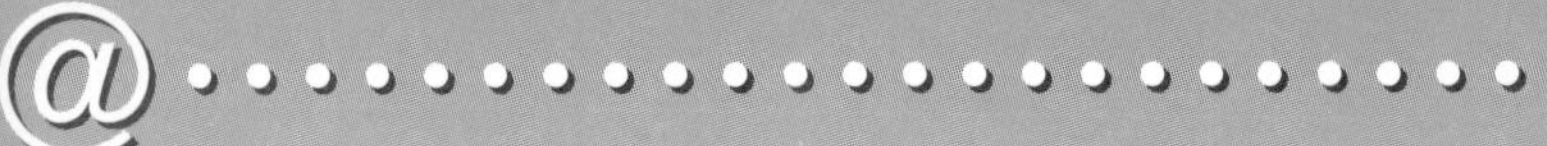

Ape Culture

http://www.apeculture.com

This strange site is dedicated to 'popular culture and the stripmall life'. It includes concert and movie reviews, celebrity news and features, all with a distinctly off-the-wall flavor.

Who's Buried Where?

http://www.findagrave.com

Do you have a burning desire to find out where Gene Kelly and other stars are buried? If so, check this out – you can even buy the T-shirt!

TV Ark

http://www.tv-ark.org.uk

Superb British TV nostalgia site with a vast array of info, pictures, theme tunes and loads more. Search by channel or by genre.

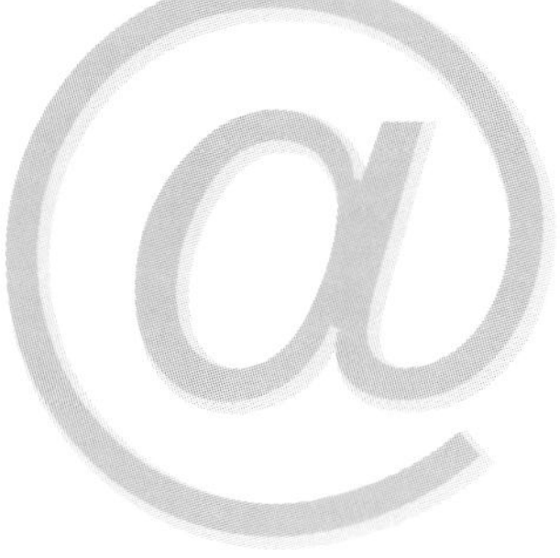

Juggle Baby!

http://www.juggling.org/movies

Did you know that over 350 known films contain scenes of juggling? What films did Robert de Niro and Johnny Depp juggle in? Log on to find out.

Celebrities Distorted

http://www.quirked.com/distortions

Countless photos of celebrity photos distorted for comic effect. Includes an A-Z search to find your favourite celeb.

6

UFOs and Aliens

Anomalous Space Images and UFOs

http://www.anomalous-images.com/index.html

Is there a face on Mars? This site offers photographs and information on this anomaly and many others.

The Center for UFO Studies

http://www.cufos.org/index.html

A general overview of UFO sightings in history – and there's even a page where you can report your very own sighting!

Famous UFO Sightings

http://ourworld.compuserve.com/homepages/AndyPage/ufosight.htm

This site contains a list of famous UFO sightings and uncovered hoaxes from as early as 1917.

UFO Watchtower

http://www.ufowatchtower.com

This purpose-built watchtower in Hooper, Colorado just might give you your best chance of spotting a flying saucer! But then again, it might not.

Cosmic Conspiracies

http://www.ufos-aliens.co.uk

A general site about UFOs and aliens – including film footage, photographs, a chat room, information on government conspiracies and the latest news.

Forbidden Science – Is There a Military Cover-up?

http://www.geocities.com/Area51/Rampart/2271

This site examines the US Military's UFO encounters and the conspiracy to keep it all quiet.

How to Fake Your Own Alien Autopsy

http://www.trudang.com/autopsy.html

A lighter look at the business of dissecting aliens – including bleeps and blunders and a 'How To Make An Alien' Handbook.

Astrobiology at NASA

http://astrobiology.arc.nasa.gov/index.cfm

For a scientific look at the anomalies of space, planets and strange objects in the sky – visit the official NASA site.

MUFON – 'The Mutual UFO Network'

http://www.mufon.com

Have you been looking for an organization to join, one that provides hotlines, trains field investigators, and even hosts an annual convention? If so, MUFON could be the network for you.

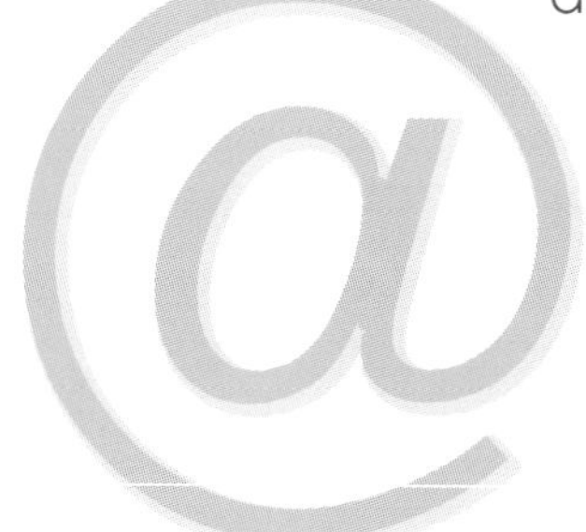

UFO Folklore

http://www.qtm.net/~geibdan/framemst.html

This site boasts an A–Z list of links and articles, including topics such as the CIA and UFOs, Mars, evidence of aliens, ancient UFOs and many more.

Above Top Secret

http://www.abovetopsecret.com

This site is dedicated to uncovering government conspiracies surrounding Area 51, aircraft projects, and the New World Order.

Saucer Smear

http://www.martiansgohome.com/smear

Reporting on the business of Ufology itself – the movers, the shakers and all the latest news and gossip.

Alien Message Board

http://www.scifichronicles.com/amb.htm

Amongst other features, there is an alien quiz, an alien shopping mall, and even an alien lonely hearts column ('Lonely, friendless, feel the need to breed? Find the alien of your dreams at the Alien Love Connection.')

The UFO Network

http://www.ufon.org

The UFO Network site charts UFO sightings from around the world. Check out the archive photos and decide for yourself whether or not they are hoaxes.

When Will We Have Warp Drives?

http://www.lerc.nasa.gov/WWW/PAO/warp.htm

Dealing with the science and technology of travelling at the speed of light, this site is a fascinating attempt to answer the question.

The Paranormal Research Primer

http://www.worldofthestrange.com

Including dozens of articles about UFO close encounters, photographs of anomalies, crop circles, alien abductions, and much much more, this vast site has it all.

UFO Abduction Insurance

http://www.ufo2001.com

This tongue-in-cheek site offers insurance against being abducted by aliens. A single lifetime premium of $19.95 will cover you to the tune of $10,000,000!

A Study of Orbs

http://www.orbsite.com/home.html

What is an orb? Well, this site contains photographic evidence so that you can find out for yourself.

International UFO Museum and Research Center

http://www.iufomrc.com

This is the homepage of a real-life museum, offering details on the Roswell Incident and research articles. It even has a gift shop where you can purchase Area 51 mugs and inflatable aliens!

UFO Art

http://dcwi.com/~talpazan/Welcome.html

Homepage of a Romanian-born artist who draws, paints and sculpts UFOs and aliens.

UFO Anomalies Zone

http://www.westol.com/~paufo

You've heard of Roswell, but probably not of Kecksburg, where the government cover-up was more successful. On this site you can find out the hushed-up truth about the giant acorn that fell from the sky.

SETI – 'The Search for Extraterrestrial Intelligence'

http://www.seti.org

The official homepage of the SETI Institute. An extremely interesting and worthy site with all the information on the current search projects – and don't forget to check out 'SETI @ Home', where you can help them search from your very own computer!

Aliens Beneath Our Feet

http://www.reptoids.com

Reptiles evolved into reptilian-humanoid beings called Reptoids which live underground. But might be able to pilot UFOs on the side.

Rearview Mirror

http://www.detnews.com/history/ufo/ufo.htm

This site tells the story of a fascinating UFO sighting on a quiet day in Michigan in 1966. The event was witnessed by over 100 people and the police even tried to chase the UFO!

Bob Lazar

http://www.boblazar.com

Bob Lazar has made many claims that he was employed at Area 51. This is his web site – perhaps he is telling the truth!

Mars For Sale

http://www.theskyisfalling.com

Own a piece of Mars for $120 plus shipping. This site will sell you a rare Martian meteorite, complete with 20-page Mars Owner's Manual. Ships worldwide.

Great Dreams

http://www.greatdreams.com/ufos.htm

Boasting links to 2,803 sites on a variety of UFO topics, this site must be visited by all fans of the 'greys'.

Zerotime

http://www.zerotime.com/ufo

Including the likely home of The Grey Aliens (Zeta 2 Reticuli) and NASA's official document explaining what procedures to follow when encountering aliens.

The UFO Museum

http://unmuseum.mus.pa.us/ufo.htm

Read about the history of strange happenings in the sky in the Hall of UFO Mysteries – a gallery of the Unnatural Museum.

The Black Vault

http://www.blackvault.com

Containing a huge list of links, this is one of the Internet's best sites on all things to do with UFOs, alien cover-ups and government conspiracies. A must-see site for die-hard UFO or conspiracy fans.

Zeta Talk

http://www.zetatalk.com

According to this site, aliens visit the Earth regularly! Discover why we are gradually getting acquainted with our visitors from outer space, and what needs to happen to allow the process to occur faster.

All About UFOs

http://ufos.about.com/mbody.htm

Get the latest news of UFO sightings around the world, by courtesy of the giant About.com web site.

Nuts About UFOs

http://www.ufonut.com

This site contains historical accounts, photos and links in an irreverent style.

Alien Dating Service?

http://www.alienlovebite.com

Ever fallen in love with someone you shouldn't have fallen in love with? It may be that an alien abducted you and programmed you to respond to another abductee. Find out all about this bizarre theory on this site.

The US National UFO Reporting Center

http://www.nwlink.com/~ufocntr

Whilst only covering the US and Canada, this site still contains some fascinating details of recent case studies including the fascinating sighting over Illinois at the start of the new millennium.

UFO Alert

http://www.UFOAlert.com

Engaged in the task of documenting UFO sightings from around the world, this site is a must-see in your quest to uncover the truth.

Meteorite Central

http://meteoritecentral.com

For the latest news and views about lumps of rock, and other things, that fall from the sky, this is the place to go. The site includes a mailing list as well as a bulletin board.

UFO City

http://www.ufocity.com

Another vast and regularly-updated site offering 'hot-off-the-press' news, many links and articles about UFOs, a bulletin board, a 'watch' campaign, and much more.

The UFO Reports' Archive

http://www.geocities.com/Area51/Rampart/2653/reports.html

In this massive archive of postings from the Alt.UFO newsgroup, you can read hundreds of reports of UFO sightings.

The Oz Files

http://www.theozfiles.com/index.html

Do UFO's fly upside down, down under? This site provides an Antipodean perspective on the UFO scene, including possible UFO connections with Australian Aboriginal culture.

Project 1947

http://www.project1947.com

Project 1947 takes a closer look at the UFO phenomenon that began at this time in our history, offering details and photographs of the main UFO sightings.

Six Inexplicable Encounters

http://popularmechanics.com/science/space/1998/7/6_ufo_sightings/

As suggested by the title, this web site takes a detailed look at six UFO encounters from around the world that have stumped the skeptics.

International UFO Congress

http://www.ufocongress.com

Would you like to know when the next UFO congress is held and how you can be updated on the discussions? Check out this site for all these details and more.

Aliens as Ancestors

http://theroad1.tripod.com

Are UFOs and aliens really our ancestors checking up on us? Visit this site for images and descriptions of extra-terrestrial encounters throughout history, and puzzling references from the Bible.

Alien Abduction

http://www.abduct.com

Personal experiences of alien abduction from all over the world are shared on this site.

Alien Fish Exchange

http://www.alienfishexchange.com

Multi-player persistent-world gaming on your cell phone. Breed the most exotic aquatic life yet discovered, then sell it to gourmet restaurants clamouring for extra-terrestrial delicacies.

The Science Behind the 'X-Files'

http://huah.net/scixf

Taking a very close look at a few episodes of the popular TV show, this site offers an explanation for the X-Files science bits. An interesting read.

The Bible UFO Connection

http://www.bibleufo.com

A web site all about the theory that God travels the skies in a UFO, and Multi-National Corporations are implicated in a plot to make us fear aliens so that we will shoot down the UFO that Jesus is going to be flying back to earth in.

The Lunar Embassy

http://www.lunarembassy.com

How would you like to buy a piece of the moon or Mars? This is precisely what this site offers.

HR Giger

http://www.hrgiger.com

This is the official site of Mr HR Giger, the genius artist who created the visual horror of the xenomorphe in the 'Alien' trilogy of movies. His art is sinister and yet beautiful – a must-see site for fans of science fiction and art.

UFO Sightings in the UK

http://www.ufosightingsuk.co.uk

A neatly designed site documenting and updating UFO sightings specific to the United Kingdom.

Alien Dave

http://www.aliendave.com/aliendave.html

A huge array of conspiracy theories are detailed on this site, most of them not surprisingly involving aliens. And a man called Dave.

Are You an Abductee?

http://www.anw.com/aliens/52questions.htm

Answer the quiz questions to find out if you are one of the select few!

Possible UFO Crash Sites and Retrievals

http://www.cseti.com/crashes/crash.htm

A huge international list of UFO crash site locations and the possible discovery of dead aliens. Has there been one near you? – log on to find out.

Alien Shopping

http://www.ufomall.com

All the alien-related merchandise you could ever need is available for purchase here!

Alien Autopsy News.

http://www.v-j-enterprises.com/jroswell.html

All the latest developments in the controversy over the Roswell Alien Autopsy tape.

The Mystical Universe

http://mysticaluniverse.com

A general site reporting various paranormal phenomena including the very latest UFO sightings, alien abductions, hauntings and NASA news.

German UFO Watch

http://www.aircooledmind.org/aliens.html

Do UFOs originate from Germany? The author of this site believes he has detected a distinct German influence in many of the space ship designs.

The Time Travel Research Center

http://www.time-travel.com

As the title suggests, this site offers fascinating information about the history, the science, and the possibilities of travelling through time.

The Paranormal News

http://www.paranormalnews.com

Updated frequently and with great video footage, this site highlights news stories about strange happenings in the sky and other paranormal events.

SARA – 'The Society of Amateur Radio Astronomers'

http://www.bambi.net/sara.html

The site to visit if you want to set up your own backyard radio telescope or just meet other like-minded people from around the globe. An excellent resource.

What Are The Triangles?

http://keyholepublishing.com/What_Are_The_Triangles.htm

This online report discusses sightings of 'impossible' crafts, and provides photos, testimonies and links to other sites discussing triangle-shaped craft.

Angry Alien

http://www.angryalien.com

This site not only shows the film, Alien being re-enacted by cartoon bunnies, but also shows other famous films featuring cartoon bunny actors!

Bad Astronomy

http://www.badastronomy.com

Explains the flawed astronomy featured in films, on TV and in the news, including discussions about The Apollo Moon Hoax, Planet X and The Face On Mars.

My Pet UFO

http://www.flying-saucer.com

Get your own radio controlled flying saucer that can even fly indoors! Choose from twin or tri turbofan models, just add helium and batteries.

Committee for the Scientific Investigation of Claims of the Paranormal

http://www.csicop.org

You can search the site for a variety of articles on UFOs and aliens, as well as other 'fringe' subjects.

Close-minded Science

http://www.amasci.com/weird/wclose.html

An interesting collection of articles about scientific skepticism generally – when to believe, when to debunk.

Alien Abduction Photos

http://www.rense.com/general32/abduct.htm

Amazing-looking photos of the aftermath of a Brazilian man being abducted from his bed through the ceiling into a spaceship.

UFO Mind

http://www.ufomind.com

Simply a vast resource of links and articles on all things UFO-related. A good place to start your own investigation.

West to Mars

http://www.marswest.org

This site gives an artistic impression of human colonization of the red planet.

Extraterrestrials – What Are They Like?

http://www.geocities.com/Area51/Shadowlands/6583/et.html

A huge site dedicated to the task of categorizing and describing alien life forms – including a series of interesting articles about the impact of aliens landing on Earth.

The Languages of Star Trek

http://www.pinette.net/chris/startrek/index.html

How do you say 'Hello!' in Ferengi, or 'Damn!' in Klingon? This site is a must for all Trekkies.

All About Alien Cultures

http://www.androidpubs.com

The web site for a manned mission to Mars, for which tickets are available now for a mere $2,000,000. The departure date is July 15, 2018, due in to Mars on August 21, 2018 if the traffic's not too bad...

Alien Alley Art Gallery

http://www.alienalley.com

Online gallery of UFO-related art. You don't have to have been abducted to exhibit here, but it helps.

Scary Aliens

http://www.xenomorph.org

This claims to be the first and largest site on the net to deal exclusively with collectibles from the Alien films. Whether you want a copy of the original movie posters or a model alien of your very own, this is the place to come!

Top Secret!

http://accelerationresearch.tripod.com

This site explores the many mysteries surrounding the Aurora, including whether it may be responsible for some presumed UFO sightings.

Roswell

http://ds.dial.pipex.com/ritson

With eye-witness accounts, stills from the famous film, and more – this unbiased site is an excellent place to find out the facts about the Roswell Incident.

Martian Mysteries

http://www.geocities.com/natethegreat2u_2000

This site contains many anomalous images from Mars that NASA didn't show the world. See the pictures here yourself and decide.

Area 51 Trip Report

http://www.nauticom.net/users/ata/area51.html

With photographs of Area 51 and various 'alleged' aircraft, this site takes an objective look at this famous conspiracy.

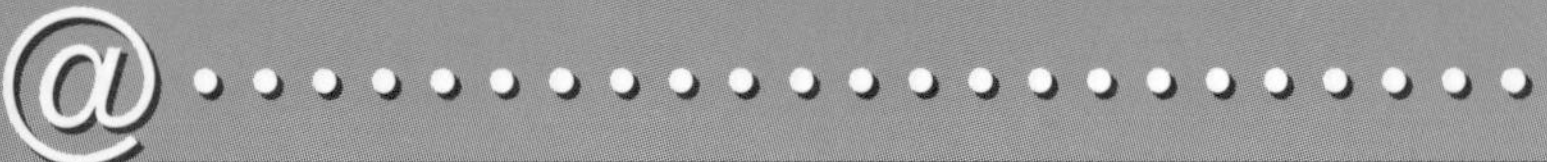

Alien Bases

http://www.karinya.com/bases1.htm

An up-to-date map of all the alien bases on Earth - really.

Atlantis

http://www.geocities.com/Area51/Corridor/2709

Could the Atlanteans have received technological information from space? Did they build the Sphinx to hide this info? Visit to find out more!

UFO Sightings by Astronauts

http://www.anomalous-images.com/astroufo.html

Many US astronauts claim to have seen UFOs during their space missions. Read about the sightings here, in some cases with previously unpublished photographs.

Afrer care

http://www.intrudersfoundation.org/acs.html

Have you been probed? Seek help here!

Unknown Country

http://www.unknowncountry.com

This is the web site of author Whitley Strieber, who famously claimed to have been abducted and experimented upon by aliens. Read here about the latest mysteries he is investigating.

LAGOON WEB SITE

Games, Books, Puzzles and Gizmos

Visit the Lagoon Web Site to view a staggering range of fantastic games, puzzles and books to suit all.

www.thelagoongroup.com

OTHER TITLES BY LAGOON BOOKS

Brain-Boosting Puzzle Books

Brain-Boosting Quantum Puzzles
(1-902813-52-9)

Brain-Boosting Cryptology Puzzles
(1-902813-54-5)

Brain-Boosting Sequence Puzzles
(1-902813-53-7)

Brain-Boosting Cryptic Puzzles
(1-902813-21-9)

Brain-Boosting Visual Logic Puzzles
(1-902813-20-0)

Brain-Boosting Lateral Thinking Puzzles
(1-902813-22-7)

OTHER TITLES IN THE SERIES:

500 of the World's Best Web Sites
ISBN: 1-902813-30-8

500 Indispensable Web Sites for Men
ISBN: 1-902813-67-7

LAGOON
BOOKS